POWER
FREEDOM
and GRACE

DEEPAK CHOPRA

POWER
FREEDOM
and GRACE

*Living from the Source of
Lasting Happiness*

AMBER-ALLEN PUBLISHING
SAN RAFAEL, CALIFORNIA

• A LIFETIME OF WISDOM •

Copyright © 2006 by Deepak Chopra

Published by Amber-Allen Publishing, Inc.
Post Office Box 6657
San Rafael, California 94903

Author Photo: Jeremiah Sullivan
Cover Illustration: Mahaveer Swami, detail from *Bhagavad Gita*

Library of Congress Cataloging-in-Publication Data

Chopra, Deepak.
Power, freedom, and grace : living from the source of lasting happiness
    p. cm.
ISBN-13: 978-1-878424-85-3 (85-3 : alk. paper)
1. Spirituality. I. Title.

BL624.C4768 2006
294.5'4--dc22   2006010817

Printed in Canada
Distributed by Hay House, Inc.

10   9   8   7   6   5   4   3

DEDICATION

To the immortal Being in all of us.

CONTENTS

ACKNOWLEDGMENTS

I am deeply grateful to Janet Mills, who has
very diligently captured the essence of my lectures
over the years, and helped me bring this
manuscript to completion.

*Do not confuse the instrument with the
user of the instrument. The instrument is the brain;
the user of the instrument is the infinite Being
expressing itself in different disguises.*

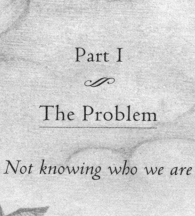

Part I

❦

The Problem

Not knowing who we are

· I ·

What do I want?

Hap · pi · ness (hăp′ ē nĭs):
A feeling of great pleasure, contentment, or joy.

There is a reason why you were drawn to this book. Perhaps your soul is extending an invitation to you — an invitation to get in touch with the deepest part of your self. Your deepest self, your essential being, is the source of all Being — the field of pure consciousness that manifests as the infinite diversity of the universe. Power, freedom, and grace are attributes of this field. So, too, are happiness, joy, and bliss.

Over the course of my career, thousands of people have come to me with various problems and challenges in their lives. My career began as a physician, and in the beginning most of the people I met had some form of illness, such as heart disease or cancer. One day I was sitting with a patient who had heart disease and I happened to ask him, "Why do you want to get better?"

The look in his eyes said, *What kind of ridiculous question is that?* He told me, "Doesn't everybody want to get better when they're sick?"

"Yes," I said, "but why do *you* want to get better?"

He replied, "If I get better, I can go back to work and make more money."

For some unknown reason, I persisted in asking him *why*. "Why do you want to make more money?"

Apparently amused, he agreed to play the game and said, "Because I want to send my son to a good university."

I asked him *why* he wanted to send his son to a good university.

He said, "I want my son to get a good education so he can build a successful career."

I kept asking him the question, *Why, why, why . . .* In the end he answered, "Because I want to be happy."

Since then, I have played this game not only with sick patients wanting to get better, but with anyone who wants anything. You can try this yourself. Ask people what they want, and when they tell you what they want, keep asking *why* until you hear the ultimate answer: "Because I want to be happy."

Happiness seems to be the goal of all other goals, and yet most people seek happiness in a roundabout way. We have material goals, such as wanting a better house, a better automobile, or items of luxury. We have goals that deal with relationship. We want to feel safe; we want to feel that we belong. We want to be able to express ourselves freely and creatively. Some of us might want wealth or power; others might seek fame. But if you ask people why they want these things, the ultimate answer remains the same: They believe that if they attain these things, *then* they will be happy.

As I talked to people, I began to have the idea, *Why not make happiness our primary goal? Why seek happiness through all these secondhand means?* And I discovered something even more interesting. If we make happiness our primary goal instead of our secondary goal, then we easily accomplish everything else we desire.

Many spiritual traditions state that if you seek the highest first, everything else comes to you. In the New Testament, for example, Christ says, "Seek first the kingdom of heaven, and all else will be added unto you." The kingdom of heaven is not some far-off place in some remote part of the universe; it is a state of consciousness. So, too, is happiness.

Most people say, "I'm happy *because* . . . because I have family and friends, because I have a great job, because I have money and security." All of these reasons for happiness are tenuous; they come and go like a passing breeze. And when happiness eludes us, we seek pleasure through addictive behaviors out of the unconscious hope that we will find joy. External causes of happiness never create real joy. Joy is an internal state of consciousness that determines how we perceive and experience the world. The internal source of joy — our connection to our Creator, our source, our inner self — is the cause, while happiness is its effect.

If you have lost touch with your internal source of joy, if the happiness you experience always originates in circumstances outside yourself, then you are at the mercy of every situation and every stranger you meet. This kind of happiness is always elusive.

Vedanta, one of the world's most ancient philosophies, tells us that happiness for a reason is just another form of misery because the reason can be taken away from us at any time. To be happy for no reason is the happiness we want to experience.

Happiness is a state of consciousness that already exists within us, but it's often covered up by all kinds of distractions. Just as a beautiful sunrise might be hidden behind the clouds, so, too, our inner happiness is hidden behind our everyday concerns. Social conditioning and constricted awareness keep us from glimpsing this kingdom of heaven hidden in the depths of our heart. But we can learn to rise above the clouds of conditioning and rediscover the source of joy deep within us. Upon discovering this joy, wonderful and miraculous things begin to happen. The expression of happiness brings a sense of connection to the creative power of the universe. Having that connection, we feel that nothing can stop us from accomplishing anything we desire.

When our life is an expression of the inner state of happiness, we discover an immense reservoir of power within us. This power gives us freedom from fear and limitations, and allows us to realize all the abundance that we aspire to. Even more significantly, this power nurtures all of our relationships and makes them truly fulfilling. We find ourselves becoming beacons of light and love, and our very presence nurtures the environment around us. People are drawn to support our desires, and even nature responds to our intentions.

The more we live in the state of happiness, the more we experience the spontaneous fulfillment of desire in the form of synchronicity and meaningful coincidence. In many spiritual traditions, this has been called the state of grace. To experience grace is to find ourselves in the right place at the right time, to have the support of the laws of nature, or "good luck." In the state of grace, it seems to us that the universal or cosmic mind is eavesdropping on our thoughts and fulfilling our intentions and desires even as we are having them.

But this is not the entire story. Though happiness is the goal of all other goals, what we really want, even beyond happiness, is to understand the mystery of our own existence. Until we do, no matter how many of our desires are fulfilled, we remain discontented because an inner voice keeps nagging at us. This voice asks, *Who am I? Where did I come from? What is the meaning and purpose of my life? Where do I go when I die?*

No one can give us the answers to these questions. If we take the answers that our parents, or our culture, or our religious traditions gave us, then we are taking whatever we learn on blind faith. When we don't know something for certain ourselves, but only *hope* that it is true, then we believe it because authority figures told us to believe it. This kind of belief is a cover-up for insecurity, and in today's age, it seems naive.

Science has given us a great deal of understanding about the laws of nature and how they work. We don't have to *believe* in electricity; we can see the evidence in a light bulb. Nor do we have to believe in the other forces of nature, such as gravity. We know that gravity exists because we can experience it. So, too, if the soul exists, if an afterlife exists, then it isn't necessary to believe in it. We don't need belief. We need understanding; we need experience. Why should we take the deepest questions of our existence on faith? Isn't there a way to find out for ourselves?

Are there means we can use to explore and understand ourselves so that we can have a direct understanding of the deep mysteries of our existence? Is it also possible for this understanding to satisfy our rationality and what we know about the universe from modern science or cosmology?

As you read this book, it is my intention that you will rediscover what you already know at a deep level, and in this act of remembrance, experience great wonder, unbounded love, and profound humility. The inner self of every human waits patiently until we are ready; then it extends an invitation to enter the luminous mystery of existence in which all things are created, nurtured, and renewed. In the presence of this mystery, we not only heal ourselves, we heal the world.

There can be no more important task in our life than to get in touch with our own inner self, the source of all Being. The deepest self within each of us is the Self of the whole universe, and it's also the source of all healing and transformation.

The world has been waiting for our transformation because it, too, wants transformation. When we are transformed, the world is transformed, because we and the world are one.

Let us start on this journey now.

❧

KEY POINTS

- Happiness is the goal of all goals, and it's a state of consciousness that already exists within you.

- Happiness for a reason is a form of misery because the reason can be taken away from you at any time. To be happy for no reason is the happiness you want to experience.

- When your life is an expression of your inner happiness, you feel a sense of connection to the creative power of the universe. Having that connection, you feel that you can accomplish anything you desire.

· 2 ·

Who am I?

U · ni · verse (y$\overline{oo}'$ nə vûrs'):
One song; the totality of all the things that exist.

According to Vedanta, there are only five reasons why humans suffer: The first is not knowing who we are. The second is identifying with our ego or self-image. The third is clinging to that which is transient and unreal. The fourth is recoiling in fear of that which is transient and unreal. And the fifth is the fear of death. Vedanta also says that the five causes of suffering are all contained in the first cause — not knowing who we are. If we can answer this one basic question, *Who am I?*, we may find the answer to all other related questions, such as: *Where did I come from? What is the meaning and purpose of my life? Where do I go when I die?*

Now, if someone were to ask, "Who are you?" your response would probably be "Oh, my name is so-and-so. I'm an American, or I'm Japanese, or I'm the president of this company." All of these answers refer to your self-image or to an object outside yourself: a name, a place, a circumstance. This process of identifying with your self-image or the objects of your experience is called *object-referral.*

You may also identify with your body and say, "This is my body. This bag of flesh and bones is who I am." But then the question is: *What is the body, and why call it yours?* The body that you call *yours* is really the raw material of the universe: recycled earth, water, and air. But so is the tree outside your window. Why call the body yours when you do not call the stars, the moon, or the tree outside your window yours?

Of course your body seems nearer to you, but this assumes that you know where the "I am" that you *think* you are is physically located.

Many people somehow feel that the "I" they call themselves, the skin-encapsulated awareness, is located somewhere in their head. Other people think it's located somewhere behind the heart or solar plexus. But no scientific experiment has ever found a center of awareness in any one location in space or time.

An interesting insight comes to us from both Vedic science and the Jewish Kabbalah: The center of our awareness is the center of all space and time. It is at once everywhere and nowhere. But let's assume for a moment that your awareness is indeed located where you are physically sitting. If this universe has infinite dimensions — and physicists assure us that it does — then infinity extends in all directions from where you are. You are in the center of the universe, but so am I, because infinity also extends in all directions from where I am. Infinity also extends in all directions from a person in China, a dog in Siberia, and a tree in Africa. The truth is, I am here, but I am also everywhere else because *here* is *there* from every other point in space. You are *there*, but you are also everywhere else because *there* is everywhere, or no-where specifically.

In other words, location in space is a matter of perception. When we say the moon is near and the sun is far, that's only true from our particular van-tage point. In reality, there is no up or down, north or south, east or west, here or there. These are only points of reference for our convenience. Everything in the cosmos is nonlocal, meaning we can't confine it to here, there, or anywhere.

But my eyes tell me this is not the case. I am here, you are there, wherever you are. So maybe we should not trust our senses that much. My eyes tell me that the Earth is flat, but nobody believes that anymore. Sensory experience tells me that the ground I am standing on is stationary, but I know from science that the Earth is spinning on its axis and hurtling through outer space at thousands of miles an hour. Sensory experience tells me that the objects of my perception are solid, but that's not true either. We know that objects are made up of atoms, which in turn are made up of particles that whirl around huge empty spaces.

The experience of a material world is a superstition that we've developed because we've learned to trust our senses. The universe is actually a chaos of energy soup, and we ingest this soup through our five senses, and then convert it into a material reality in our consciousness. Our senses transform massless energy into sound and vibration, form and solidity, texture and color, fragrance and taste. And our interpretation of that energy soup structures our reality and creates our perceptual experience. Most of the time we do this unconsciously as a result of social conditioning. Philosophers have called this *the hypnosis of social conditioning*. When we live under this hypnosis, we believe *the superstition of materialism.*

The superstition of materialism relies on sensory experience as the crucial test of reality. In this worldview, reality is what we can see with our eyes, hear with our ears, smell with our nose, taste with our mouth, or touch with our hands. If energy or information is not available to our senses, we tend to think it isn't there. And the intellect, with its linguistically structured system of logic, serves to justify this mistaken perception of reality.

Sensory experience is totally illusory; it's as transient as a fantasy or a dream. Is there really such a thing as the color red? Every color you see is a particular wavelength of light, and the light you can actually detect is a fraction of what exists. How long can you cling to a world of illusion? You may think you are the body that your senses can locate in space and time, but the body is a field of invisible vibrations that has no boundaries in space and time.

So maybe you are not the image you identify with, and maybe you are not the body. Then at least you must be your thoughts and feelings. But who can honestly claim to know where thoughts and feelings come from? Where do they come from, and where do they disappear?

If you can't claim exclusivity over the objects of your experience, your body, or even your thoughts and feelings, then what can you call your own? And here the knowledge of Vedanta saves us. If you replace the word *exclusive* with the word *inclusive*, then you are not *just* these objects, you are not *just* this body, you are not *just* these thoughts and feelings. You are *all* things, you are *all* bodies, you are *all* thoughts and feelings. You are a field of all possibilities.

The essential you, your *real* essence, is a field of awareness that interacts with its own self and then becomes both mind and body. In other words, you are consciousness or spirit, which then conceives, constructs, governs, and becomes the mind and the body. The real you is inseparable from the patterns of intelligence that permeate every fiber of creation.

At the deepest level of existence, you are Being, and you are nowhere and everywhere at the same time. There is no other "you" than the entire cosmos. The cosmic mind creates the physical universe, and the personal mind experiences the physical universe.

But in truth, the cosmic mind and the personal mind are both permeated by infinite consciousness. Infinite consciousness is our source, and all manifestation is inherent within it.

Infinite consciousness observing itself creates the notion of observer, or the soul; the process of observation, or the mind; and that which is observed, or the body and the world. The observer and the observed create relationships between themselves; this is space. The movement of these relationships creates events; this is time. But all of these are none other than the infinite consciousness itself.

In other words, we are infinite consciousness with a localized point of view. And yet our whole system of thought divides the observer from the observed; it divides the infinite consciousness into a world of objects separated by space and time. The intellect imprisons us in a cage of fictitious images, a suffocating web of space, time, and causation. As a result, we lose touch with the true nature of our reality, which is powerful, boundless, immortal, and free.

We are all prisoners of the intellect. And the intellect's mistake in one simple sentence is this: It mistakes the *image* of reality for reality itself. It squeezes the soul into the volume of a body, into the span of a lifetime, and the spell of mortality is cast. The *image* of the self overshadows the unbounded Self, and we feel cut off or disconnected from infinite consciousness, our source. This is the beginning of fear, the onset of suffering, and all of the problems of humanity, from our minor insecurities to our major catastrophes, such as war, terrorism, and all other acts of human degradation. To one who is trapped in the prison of the intellect, all is indeed suffering. But the cause of this suffering can be averted. Ignorance of our real nature causes the inner self to be obscured. But when ignorance is destroyed, the powerful, unbounded nature of the inner self is revealed.

At first this may sound strange and abstract, but as you bear with this notion and understand it, you realize the most dramatic discovery: The real you is nonmaterial and therefore not subject to the limitations of space, time, matter, and causation. The soul, the spirit, the essential you, is beyond all that. In this very moment, you are surrounded by a field of pure consciousness. Pure consciousness illuminates and animates your mind and body, and it is powerful, nourishing, invincible, unbounded, and free. Pure consciousness, the eternal spirit, animates everything in existence, which means it is omniscient (all-knowing), omnipresent (present in all locations simultaneously), and omnipotent (all-powerful).

Now, if you don't fully comprehend this, don't worry about it. In the following chapters we will take a closer look at the different expressions of the spirit, the inner self, the source of all that is. As you read these pages, you will get a better understanding of who you really are. Once you have fully grasped this understanding, your life will be established in joy. Not only will you have the power to accomplish all that you want, but you will also have true freedom and grace. This means you will never experience fear, not even the fear of death.

∽

KEY POINTS

- You are a field of awareness; your real essence is pure consciousness, or spirit, which becomes both the mind and the body.

- The intellect mistakes the *image* of reality for reality itself, and this image overshadows the *real* you.

- When you identify with your real essence, you escape the prison of the intellect, and enter the world of the infinite, unbounded, and free.

· 3 ·

Why do I forget who I am?

∽

Su · per · sti · tion (sōo′ pər stĭsh′ ən):
A belief based on fear or ignorance of the laws of nature.

What is this thing that we call our *body;* what is this thing that we call our *mind?* As we will see, our traditional ideas of the body and mind are based on obsolete notions or *superstitions* that we've learned to believe in. Sensory experience and social conditioning cause us to forget who we are. There is a deeper reality to the body; there is a deeper reality to the mind. And that deeper reality is what we want to experience, because out of that reality come both the body and the mind.

Quantum physics tells us that the world is composed of one underlying field of intelligence that manifests as the infinite diversity of the universe. The field of intelligence experienced subjectively is the mind; the same field experienced objectively is the world of material objects. Mind and matter are not separate entities; mind and matter are essentially the same. Our essential being, stripped of the superficial layers of mind and body, is neither mind nor matter but the source of both. In other words, the human body is the human mind at the same time. We are actually a body-mind; we can't really separate the two. Nor can we confine the mind to the brain or even to the body, because the mind extends beyond our body into the whole universe.

The superstition of materialism says the human body is a solid clump of matter separated from other objects in space and time. But "solid" objects are not solid at all, nor are they separate from one another in space and time. Objects are focal points, or concentrations of intelligence, within the field of intelligence. At the most fundamental levels of nature, there are no well-defined edges between our personal body and that of the universe. Knowing this frees us from the hallucination of a separate self that lives inside a separate body.

If we could see the body through the eyes of a physicist, as it *really* is, we'd see a huge empty void with a few scattered dots and some random electrical discharges. The body is made up of atoms, which in turn are made up of particles that whirl at dizzying speeds around huge empty spaces. Physicists have fancy names for these particles, such as *leptons, quarks, mesons,* and so on. These particles give us the experience of matter through our senses, but they are definitely not material entities. These particles are fluctuations of information and energy existing in a huge void. The particles constantly emerge from the void, come into creation, rebound, collide, and then disappear back into the void.

The field of intelligence responsible for the material expression of the body is mostly quantum fluctuations in empty space. The human body *itself* is mostly empty space, but that empty space is not an emptiness made up of nothing; it is a fullness of nonmaterial intelligence. It is pure consciousness.

The essential point is that our real nature is a nonmaterial field of intelligence. Some scientists call this essential ground of our being *the unified field,* because it's the field of the whole universe. And when this field of intelligence thinks and interacts with itself, the material world comes out as its expression.

The superstition of materialism sees the human body as a frozen sculpture fixed in space and time, but the body-mind is actually a changing, pulsating pattern of intelligence. It is a river of energy and information — a fluid, dynamic, and ceaselessly changing pattern of energy that constantly re-creates itself. The Greek philosopher Heraclitus said, "You cannot step into the same river twice because new water is flowing in." Likewise, we cannot step into the same body twice because in every second of our existence our personal body is exchanging energy and information with our extended body, the universe.

If we take any process — such as breathing, eating, digestion, metabolism, even thought, which is fundamentally a fluctuation of energy and information in the body — we see how dramatically, how rapidly, and how effortlessly we renew our body in every second of our existence.

With each breath we inhale billions of atoms that ultimately end up as heart cells, kidney cells, brain cells, and so on. With each breath we exhale bits and pieces of our tissues and organs and exchange them with the atmosphere of this planet. Radioactive isotope studies show that the body replaces 98 percent of all its atoms in less than one year. The body makes a new stomach lining every five days, a new skin once every month, a new liver every six weeks, and a new skeleton every three months. Even our DNA, the genetic material that holds memories of billions of years of evolution, wasn't the same six weeks ago.

So if you think you are your physical body, which body are you talking about? The body you have today is not the same one you had three months ago.

The superstition of materialism sees the body as a physical machine that has somehow learned how to think, but in fact infinite consciousness somehow creates the mind and then expresses itself as the body. The body is a pattern of intelligence in a field of pure consciousness. Out of this field of consciousness, this mostly "empty space" of our body, emerge thoughts, feelings, and emotions, which then become the molecules of the body.

Thought, at a primordial level, is an impulse of energy and information, and it comes from the field of pure consciousness. Thought is that faint impulse we experience all the time in our awareness, motivating us to drink a glass of water or to walk from here to there. But it's not just a thought; it's a feeling, a desire, an instinct, a drive, a notion, an idea. At this level of existence, as we think, we make molecules, and scientific research has shown how true this is.

When we have a thought or a feeling, our brain makes a set of chemicals known as *neuropeptides* — *neuro* because they were first found in the brain; *peptides* because they are protein-like molecules. This is how brain cells speak to one another — not in the English language, but in the language of chemical messengers from inner space. Scientists tell us that there are receptors to these chemical messengers on the surface of brain cells. When a brain cell wants to speak to another brain cell, it manufactures neuropeptides that latch onto the receptor sites on other brain cells. So to think is to practice brain chemistry.

But when scientists look elsewhere in the body, they find receptors to these chemical messengers that are the equivalent of thought in other parts of the body. These receptors are not only in brain cells but in stomach cells, in heart cells, in colon cells, in kidney cells, and so on throughout the body. Stomach cells, heart cells, and other cells generate the same chemicals that the brain makes when it thinks. So we have a thinking body.

We can't imprison the mind in the brain; the mind is in every cell of the body. When we say, "I have a sad heart" or "I'm bursting with joy," we're speaking truthfully, because that is what's happening at the chemical level, the most fundamental level, in a cell. Or when we say, "I have a gut feeling about something," we're not speaking metaphorically, we're speaking literally, because our gut makes the same chemicals that our brain makes when it thinks. In fact, our gut feeling may be more accurate than our intellect, because presumably gut cells have not yet evolved to the stage of self-doubt.

When we're feeling tranquil, our body is making a tranquilizer similar to the one drug companies make, only it doesn't make us feel like a zombie. When we're feeling anxious, our body is making jittery molecules, and they're not just made in the adrenal glands; they're made everywhere in the body. When we're feeling exhilarated, our body is making immunomodulators that act as powerful anticancer drugs. The cells of our immune system, which protect us from cancer, infectious disease, and degenerative disorders, also have receptors to chemical messengers that are the material equivalent of thought. The immune system is a circulating nervous system; it's intelligent, and it's moving around in the body. So we can't have a thought, or a feeling, or a desire without our immune cells knowing about it. The immune cells are actually eavesdropping on our internal dialogue.

When we're thinking, when we're dreaming, when we're just having the vaguest impulse of intelligence in our awareness, the immune cells are listening and making the same chemicals the brain makes when it thinks. The immune cells are conscious little beings with their own notions, their own intelligence, their own emotions.

Now this might sound very esoteric to you, but it's a scientific fact. You have a thinking immune system that knows how to discriminate between a friendly bacterium and an unfriendly bacterium, between a carcinogen and a harmless chemical. When your body encounters a bacterium, even though it has never encountered that bacterium before, it remembers the first time a human encountered that bacterium in the evolutionary history of the species, and it makes the precise antibody for that bacterium.

You have an inner pharmacy that is absolutely exquisite. You name it — the body can make it in the right dose, at the right time, for the right organ, with no side effects, and all the instructions are contained in the packaging. This capacity demonstrates profound intelligence, and in fact your whole body is this field of intelligence.

But what does all this have to do with power, freedom, and grace? If you really understood that who you are is the same field of intelligence that creates the body, the mind, and the entire cosmos — if you could know this intellectually and experientially — then why would you not have the power to manifest? Why would you not have the freedom of unbounded consciousness? How could you *not* live in grace? If you really understood who you are, then what part of pure consciousness would be unavailable to you? You would know your own self as the observer and the observed, the dancer and the dance, the desire and its fulfillment. You would know that you are a field of pure potentiality with the power of creation.

There is an ancient saying from India: "Going back within myself, I create again and again. I create the mind, I create the body, I create perceptions, I create the universe. I create all those things that I call reality."

Once you know that your body-mind is a field of pure consciousness, you no longer cling to the transient and unreal. You no longer recoil in fear of it either. You feel free as a leaf in the wind, as free as the wind itself. And there is nothing more valuable than the freedom of pure, unbounded consciousness. This freedom, this liberation, is enlightenment.

Vedanta declares, "Know that one thing by knowing which everything else is known." For one who knows the Self, the limitations of the world disappear.

∽

Key Points

- You forget who you are because you have been socially conditioned to trust your senses and to believe in the superstition of materialism.

- You are inseparable from the field of intelligence that creates the entire cosmos. Knowing this frees you from the hallucination of a separate self that lives inside a separate body.

- When you realize that your body-mind is a field of pure consciousness, then you know that you have power, freedom, and grace. Therefore, happiness is knowing your true nature, which is all of these things.

· 4 ·

How do I participate in creating my reality?

❧

Cau · sa · tion (kô zā' shən):
The act of causing; anything producing an effect.

Our senses tell us that events happen within space and time. There is a past, present, and future, and the world operates through linear cause-effect relationships. So every time I make a choice, I cause an effect, and that effect becomes the cause of another effect. Things have to happen one at a time. I have to walk from here to there, from one location to another. This causes a timeline to appear.

That is how our senses experience the world, but in fact the world is not like that. The world is synchronistic, it's coincidental, it's happening simultaneously. Infinite possibilities coexist at the same time. Everything is happening all at once, and everything is correlated and instantly synchronized with everything else. This simultaneity can only happen through what is called *infinite correlation*. Infinite correlation is the ability to do an infinite number of things and correlate them with one another at the same time.

The human body is the best example of infinite correlation because it's a field of simultaneity where physics, chemistry, biology, and mathematics all come together to create the experience of life. The body has a hundred trillion cells, which is more than all the stars in the Milky Way galaxy. Each cell is doing countless things per second, and it instantly knows what the other cells are doing and correlates its activity with all the other cells. There's no *time* for one cell to tell another cell, "Listen, I'm going to digest food; you wait a while, and don't think thoughts for now."

Our stomach cells are digesting food, while our brain cells are thinking thoughts, while our gallbladder is making bile, while our immune system is killing germs. The cells not only do more than one thing at a time, but they all keep track of what the others are doing; otherwise there would be a great deal of confusion in the body.

At the same time that it's correlating all these activities, our body is monitoring the movement of the Earth, the moon, the planets, the stars, and the entire cosmos. Our body, our mind, our emotions — everything in our physiology is changing moment to moment, depending on the time of the day, the cycles of the moon, the seasons, and even the tides.

Our body is part of the universe, and everything that happens in the universe ultimately affects the physiology of our body. Biological rhythms are an expression of the rhythms of the Earth in relationship to the entire cosmos, and four of these rhythms — daily rhythms, tidal rhythms, monthly or lunar rhythms, and annual or seasonal rhythms — are the basis of all of the other rhythms in our body.

As the Earth spins on its axis, we experience a twenty-four-hour cycle of night and day that we call *the circadian rhythm*. This rhythm is based on the spinning of the Earth, and everything in our body, being part of the Earth, is also spinning and following the rhythm of the Earth. When this biological rhythm is disrupted by long-distance travel, for example, we experience jet lag. Or if we work a night shift, we don't feel quite right even if we rest during the day, because our biological rhythms are out of tune with the cosmic rhythms.

Scientific data shows that if we give an animal a certain dose of radiation at one time of the day, it may have a beneficial effect. If we give the same dose of radiation twelve hours later, the animal may die. Why? Because its physiology has changed completely in that twelve-hour period. Even a little bit of sub-jective experience tells us that at certain times of the day we feel hungry, while at other times of the day we feel sleepy. We know that we tend to feel one way at four o'clock in the afternoon, and another way at four o'clock in the morning.

Tidal rhythms also have an effect on our physiology. These rhythms are the result of the gravitational effect of the sun, the moon, and the stars in the distant galaxies on the oceans of planet Earth. We have an ocean within us that is similar to the oceans of our planet. More than 60 percent of our body is water, and more than 60 percent of our planet is water. So we experience a low tide and a high tide, and the tides ebb and flow in our own physiology. When we feel out of sorts, our body is out of synch with the body of the universe. Spending time near the ocean, or anywhere in nature, can help us to synchronize our rhythms with nature's rhythms.

The lunar rhythm is a twenty-eight-day cycle that occurs as a result of the movement of the Earth, the sun, and the moon in relationship to one another. This rhythm is evident in the waxing and waning of the moon. We see the full moon, the half moon, no moon, and then the cycle starts all over again. Human fertility and menstruation are good examples of lunar rhythms, and there are many other twenty-eight-day cycles. When I worked as a physician in an emergency room, we would frequently expect to see patients with certain types of problems depending on the time of day and the cycles of the moon.

As the Earth moves around the sun, we experience seasonal rhythms as distinct biochemical changes in the body-mind. So we are more likely to fall in love in spring or get depressed in winter. People with a condition known as seasonal affective disorder get depressed in winter but feel better when you expose them to sunlight. Seasonal changes affect not only the biochemistry of the human body; they affect the biochemistry of trees, flowers, butterflies, bacteria, and everything throughout nature.

The Earth tilts on its axis in the spring, and flowers bloom, groundhogs come out of the ground, birds migrate, fish return to their spawning grounds, and mating rituals begin. People are moved to write poetry, lovers sing songs, and young and old hearts fall in love. Seasonal rhythms affect us biologically, mentally, emotionally, and it all has to do with the relationship of the Earth to the sun.

There are other cycles and rhythms that oscillate for just a few seconds, including electrocardiogram and brain waves, and there are rhythms that last anywhere from thirty minutes to twenty-eight hours called *ultradian rhythms*. There are cycles within cycles, and it gets very complicated, but it's all one symphony. All of these rhythms create the symphony of the universe, and the body-mind is always trying to synchronize its rhythms with the rhythms of the universe.

To separate the body-mind from the rest of the cosmos is to misperceive things as they really are. The body-mind is part of a larger mind, it's part of the cosmos, and cosmic rhythms result in profound changes in our physiology. The universe is truly a symphony of the stars. And when our body-mind is in synch with this symphony, everything is spontaneous and effortless, and the exuberance of the universe flows through us in joyful ecstasy.

The real expression of the body-mind is this field of intelligence that pervades every cell, that correlates all of these activities with one another, and that does all of this below the level of our conscious awareness. Scientists might call this expression of the body-mind *infinite correlation*. But if we are not scientists, we might call these qualities of the body-mind *omniscient, omnipresent,* and *omnipotent.*

While it may sound as if I'm speaking in mystical terms, in scientific terms this is an accurate statement. What could be a more dramatic example of omniscience, omnipresence, and omnipotence? The mind knows everything all at once, it is everywhere all at once, and it is all-powerful. As part of a vast field of intelligence, the mind extends far beyond the reaches of the cosmos. Though it might find expression in localized forms and phenomena, the mind is nonlocal, which means it can't be confined to one location.

Time, too, is nonlocal. The fact that we can localize time is just a perceptual artifact based on the quality of our attention. This moment is at the center of eternity, but so is every other moment because eternity extends backward and forward from every other moment. There is no past or future, then or now, before or after; there is only the eternal moment. All that is experienced is experienced in present-moment awareness — in the here and now, and nowhere else.

We tend to think that there's such a thing as time, but ask any physicist, "Is time a thing or a notion? Does time really exist, or is it just a concept to explain the experience of change in our environment?" An eminent quantum physicist, once said, "No experiment has ever been done that proves the existence of time." Time is not a thing; time is an *idea*.

Physicists no longer use the word *time;* they use the term *space-time continuum* because they know that time is a relative phenomenon; it's not absolute. The movement of planet Earth spinning on its axis and hurtling around the sun at thousands of miles per hour creates our experience of time. But time is an illusion; it's an internal dialogue we use to explain our experience or perception of change and relationship.

Consciousness is infinite, unbounded, and eternal, which means it has no beginning, it has no end, and it has no edges or boundaries in time. How do you measure something that's infinite? You can't measure it. All measuring is conceptual, and infinity is beyond our conception. So we can say that time is the way consciousness measures the space or gap between one experience and another. In measuring itself, consciousness creates the experience of time and also the experience of space. The space-time continuum creates the experience of cause and effect, and this creates the experience of the material world.

How does all of this apply to us? Well, the way we *interpret* the concept of time — how we *metabolize* our experience of time — brings about distinct physiological changes in the body-mind. This is a fascinating aspect of our biology. Let me give you a few examples.

The circadian rhythm, which controls the cycles of sleep and rest, appetite and elimination, is easily disrupted by traveling across different time zones. Yet once while I was on a flight from Boston to London,

I met an old friend. We were having such a good time that "time flew." The flight took six or seven hours, but for us it seemed like we arrived, as the expression goes, "in a jiffy." We forgot to sleep, we forgot to eat, we forgot to go to the bathroom. When we arrived in London, we didn't even have jet lag. What happened in our case? Well, because of this faint notion that "time was flying," our biology was unaffected by the change in time zones.

Many experiments have shown that our interpretation of time influences our biology. For example, what does the word *Monday* mean to you? An astonishing fact is that more people die in our culture on Monday mornings at nine o'clock than at any other time of the week. That's a stunning accomplishment for which only the human species can take credit. Presumably no other animal knows the difference between Monday and Tuesday. And what is the difference? The difference is an idea, a notion, a thought — what Monday means to us or how we *interpret* it. There are people who say "I'm running out of time" because they have ten deadlines to meet. They are constantly trying to "beat time." They look at the same clock that you and I are looking at, but for them it's moving faster as a result of their internal perception of time. If you measure their biological responses, you find that their heart rates are faster, their blood pressure is higher, their insulin levels are higher, and they have more heart arrhythmias per minute. And when they suddenly drop dead of a heart attack, time has indeed run out for them. They have converted their internal experience of time running out into the physical experience of time running out.

There are other people whose perception, internal dialogue, and interpretation of time is "I have all the time in the world." And we find that their heart rate is slower, their blood pressure is lower, their biological responses are much smoother, and they live longer.

Then there are moments when time seems to come to a standstill, as in "The beauty of the mountain was breathtaking. *Time stood still.*" When time stands still, thought comes to a standstill. When thought comes to a standstill, the experience of change in the body comes to a standstill. In fact, what scientists call *entropy,* or aging, also stops in those moments because aging is, in part, an expression of how we metabolize or interpret time.

As a resident doctor, I worked in a psychiatric ward, and I noticed that some of the patients with psychoses had no concept of time. As a result, their bodies didn't seem to age. I saw a sixty-year-old woman who looked as if she were thirty years old. There were many such individuals. Why? Because even the concept of time didn't exist for them, and time is a concept to begin with.

So to bring this back to practical terms, all of these different experiences of time are nothing more than interpretations in our consciousness. How we interpret time, how we interpret space, how we interpret physical reality determines our experience of physical reality, including the experience of the physical body. Our body is the metabolic end product of our sensory experiences and our *interpretation* of these sensory experiences. How do you experience time or change? If you are always in a hurry and always trying to beat time or compete with time, you are causing those hurried types of changes in your biology. On the other hand, if your interpretation of time is truer to reality, which is, in fact, that there is only an eternal present, then your biology will reflect that truer notion.

In the present, you can experience the past; in the present, you can anticipate the future. But if you can *stay* in the present, if you can *be* with the present, then even the physical changes that normally occur with the passage of time will not occur in your body. There is a saying from a Vedic master: "The only reason people grow old and die is that they see other people growing old and dying."

What we see, we become; what we touch, we become. Even our memories are constantly transforming themselves into physical reactions in our body. Our interpretation of reality, our interpretation of our body-mind, generates all kinds of biochemical reactions inside us. These interpretations become memories, and the memories spontaneously trigger transformations without our knowing it. And where are these memories located? These memories are everywhere. They are nonlocally present in our soul, they manifest in our brain cells, and they get encoded in every cell of our body.

Your body is a field of ideas, and the body you're experiencing right now is an expression of all of the ideas you have about it. If you have the idea that your body is a physical machine, that it's supposed to age in a certain way, that it gets imbalanced because of environmental changes, all of these ideas translate into chemical changes in the body. If these ideas change, and they *will* change according to scientific discovery, then just that change in how you *view* the body will spontaneously cause transformations in the body.

As a pattern of intelligence in a vast field of intelligence, you participate in creating the world you experience. The world "out there" may appear to be objective, but in fact the world is subjective; it is a construct of your own interpretations. You learn to interpret the world through your senses, and this brings about your perceptual experiences, including your experience of the body-mind.

An interesting example of how the body-mind interprets, participates in, and constructs its own experience is the placebo response. Years ago, doctors discovered that they could give people unmedicated sugar pills, tell them that the pills would kill their pain, and a certain number of patients, approximately 30 percent, would experience relief from their pain. This became known as the *placebo response*.

Then it was discovered that placebo responses occur not only in pain syndromes but in other conditions. So if doctors give patients a pill and say, "This is going to relieve your heart disease," that simple notion in their awareness as a true idea causes them to make a chemical that has the effect of lowering their blood pressure and improving the flow of blood to their heart.

The placebo response is important to our understanding of the body-mind connection because the placebo response is basically an *interpretation* we make to ourselves. We don't need to use affirmations; we just have a simple notion, "This is going to relieve my pain," and the body-mind brings this about by making these very powerful chemicals.

Now, the opposite of the placebo response is the *nocebo* response. Let's say a patient walks into a doctor's office and the doctor says, "Mrs. Smith, I'm sorry to tell you, but you have breast cancer that has metastasized to all your bones. You have only six months to live." If Mrs. Smith happens to believe everything her doctor tells her, she may translate this notion into that outcome. And what is the nocebo response? Just another interpretation we make to ourselves.

To realize the power of interpretation is to acquire a new definition of the body-mind. We can do wonderful things with this body. We can evoke the healing response from within because we have an inner pharmacy that can make the appropriate drugs. We can restructure our perception of time, which would completely restructure the physical expression of the body, so it would even be possible to retard or reverse the aging process.

The human body-mind is part of a conscious, thinking field of intelligence. In every second of our existence, the local expression that we call *the body-mind* is exchanging energy and information with the nonlocal expression that we call *the universe*. The only thing is, we are doing it unconsciously. The average person thinks about sixty thousand thoughts a day. This is not surprising. But it's a little disconcerting that 95 percent of the thoughts we have today are the same ones we had yesterday. Every day we unconsciously create the same energy patterns that give rise to the same physical expression of the body.

Imagine that you could change the bricks of a building once a year, but through force of habit or because you didn't know any better, you were stuck with the notion that there was only one way to create the building. So you'd put the bricks in the same places year after year, and you'd get the same kind of building. Well, if you have the notion that the body is supposed to weaken, age, or become ill with the passing of time, this notion is translated into those energy patterns.

Every interpretation we make in every moment has an effect on the energy patterns of our body. And we can change our interpretations because *we* made them in the first place. We have the power to make choices. But most people are victims of societal thinking; they are under the hypnosis of social conditioning. Our senses take in less than one billionth of the stimuli available to us, and our social conditioning reinforces what we think is possible, editing out what we don't think is possible. We have to wake up and go beyond this hypnosis; we have to go beyond social conditioning to a deeper level. How can we do this? By witnessing the whole process and becoming conscious of it. Then we realize that there are choices.

Imagine that your nervous system is the hardware, and all the chemical changes that occur in your body are the software. The software, or program, changes according to your thoughts, feelings, interpretations, and desires. But there is a programmer. Who is the programmer? The programmer is the inner self, the *silent witness*, the ever-present awareness that witnesses everything. And when you get in touch with the silent witness, this gives you the ability to rewrite the program.

As the silent witness, you recognize that you are the thinker of every thought. When you say, "I have an idea about such and such," the "I" implies a thinker behind the thought. That thinker, the silent witness, is in the silent gap between your thoughts. It can't be found in either the body or the mind because it's beyond both body and mind. Between every thought is a little gap of silence, and that's where you'll find the *real* you. That gap is the corridor, the window, the transformational vortex through which you, the personal mind, communicate with the cosmic mind.

The silent witness is the programmer, the one who has the insights, the one who makes the choices. The silent witness is the one part of you that doesn't change. If you find the part of you that *doesn't* change, then you'll be able to cause transformation in the part of you that *does* change. And you don't have to do it by stating affirmations that your body is this, or your body is that. You don't have to brainwash yourself about anything. You just need to have the understanding or the insight to spontaneously cause transformation in your body.

To become familiar with the miracle of the human body-mind is to acquire awesome power. This power is magical because it allows you to experience the body-mind as more fluid, more flexible, more dynamic, and more creative than you have ever imagined. But first you have to understand your true nature; you have to know the body-mind as it really is.

The field of pure consciousness creates, controls, and constantly becomes the body-mind. Get in touch with this field, and you have a completely new reality of the mind and a completely new experience of the body. You realize that you can change your body more effortlessly, more rapidly, more efficiently than you can change your clothes.

⌒

KEY POINTS

- You participate in creating your reality by interpreting your sensory experience. The world is a construct of your own interpretations.

- The human body is a field of ideas, and the body you experience is an expression of all the ideas you have about it.

- When the rhythms of your body-mind are in synch with nature's rhythms, everything is effortless and the universe flows through you in joyful ecstasy.

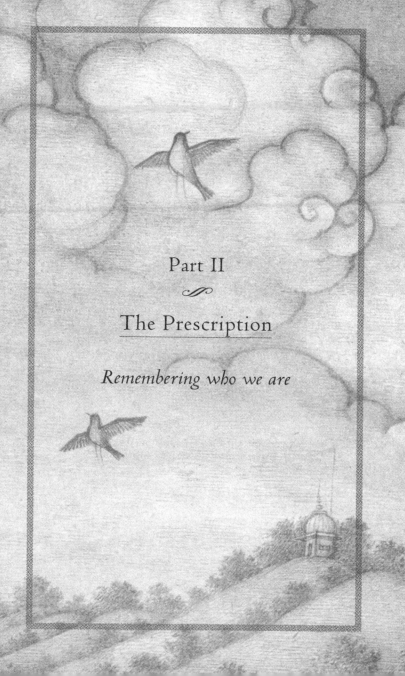

Part II

The Prescription

Remembering who we are

· 5 ·

Where do I go when I die?

✐

*Dis · con · ti · nu · i · ty (dĭs kŏn' tə nōō' ĭtē):
Lack of continuity, a gap or break.*

So now we have answered that basic question we started out with: *Who am I?* And the answer is: *I am pure consciousness, pure potentiality, a field of all possibilities.* That's who I am. I am not the body, nor am I the mind. I am the one who has the body and the one who has the mind. Spirit, the one Being, is becoming all of that, and that essence is omniscient, omnipresent, and omnipotent.

So the next question is: *Where did I come from?* And the answer to that is: *I did not come from anywhere, because I was always here.* The body comes and goes, but "I" am always here. Where I come from is a place that has no beginning in time and no ending. Where I go is the same place. As we have seen, there are no particular locations in space or time. In a nonlocal universe, there is nowhere to go!

And *what is my purpose in life?* To be happy, to joyfully participate in the creativity and evolution of the universe. Life is conceived and imagined by universal spirit, or consciousness, and all realms are imaginary forms of the spirit, which is doing its *leela*, or play. In the end, all is the play of consciousness, or *leela*.

And *what happens to me when I die?* The answer: *Nothing happens, because I do not die.* Pure consciousness cannot be destroyed; it can only be expressed. Knowing this frees us from the fear of death because nothing in the universe is ever lost; it is only transformed. If you and I are speaking on the phone, and somebody cuts off the phone lines, what happens to us?

Where do we go? Nothing happens to us, and we don't go anywhere. So, too, when physical death occurs, nothing happens to us. Certain lines of communication that use a certain nervous system have temporarily been disrupted. But we are still here. The soul doesn't go anywhere; it's the body that dissolves and returns to the earth.

Then where is the soul? One of the biggest misconceptions is that the soul resides in the body. People may say, "This person died, and the soul has left," but it's not true. The soul is not inside the body. The soul projects itself as the body and the mind. It finds a location in space-time, and broadcasts or telecasts itself through the body. But just as the characters in a movie are not inside my television set when I'm watching it, and Beethoven is not inside my radio when I'm listening to it, my soul is not inside my body. My soul is merely localizing or expressing itself through my body.

If we go to a bookstore, we can find numerous books on so-called "out-of-body" experiences. The real mystery is how we get an "in-body" experience.

To believe that our soul is "inside a body, looking out" is a convincing but socially induced hallucination.

The soul doesn't exist in space or time; it is beyond space and time. Yet everything we call *physical* seems to occupy some little place in space-time. The chair we sit on is localized in a particular spot, and for a period of time. Our body occupies different locations in space-time. Our thoughts occupy different locations in space-time, and all this is the localization of our soul, which has no location in space-time. We can therefore say that the soul is transcendent.

So when we ask, *Where is the soul?*, we're not asking the right question because *where* implies a location in space-time. The soul is everywhere and nowhere at the same time. It's everywhere in general, and nowhere in particular.

If we go beyond the superstition of materialism, we can see that our body-mind is a field of intelligence, of unconditional life force. The life force expresses itself through infinite transformations into this or that form, into this or that phenomenon, now appearing, now disappearing. But the life force itself is eternal; it's unchanging, it's all-pervading, and we are that force.

The most outstanding characteristic of this field of intelligence is its aliveness. It is the life force of the universe interacting with itself and manifesting as the exquisite dance of creation, maintenance, and dissolution, or renewal. These three forces are operating everywhere in nature.

If we look at a quantum field, we see a particle emerge from the void. That's the creative act. Then it becomes a wave in the field. That's the moment of attention when it appears for a short period of time. Then it disappears back into the void. This is the dissolution, or renewal. Throughout nature, we see that things are created and renewed, but for renewal to take place, the old must go. And in fact we are constantly re-creating ourselves at the quantum mechanical level, the atomic level, the molecular level, the material level of the physical body.

The universe, though it is timeless and eternal, functions through cycles of rest and activity — on and off. On and off means birth and death, and we are constantly dying in order to re-create ourselves. The atoms in our body go on and off. The molecules of our skin cells go on and off, dying once a month so we can make new ones. If our skin cells didn't die once a month, we would have very leathery, unhealthy skin.

Though the world appears to be continuous, in reality it's going on and off like a flashing neon sign. Everything is vibrating, and vibration implies an on-off signal. That's why it's called a *vibration*. If we could see the world at the level of photons, it would be on-off, on-off. Even our thoughts are clusters of photons flickering in and out of the infinite void. Some things vibrate very fast, some a little more slowly. In a rock, the vibration is very slow; in a thought, it's very fast; and at the level of photons, it's at the speed of light. But it's all an on-off vibration.

When we go on, we are born; when we go off, we die. Without the off, there would be no on. In every off, the universe re-creates itself. The off is also called *the discontinuity*. In our consciousness, we create the experience of continuity out of something that is essentially a discontinuity. The reason the universe appears continuous is a trick of our senses. Our senses cannot process information that flickers in and out of the infinite void at the speed of light, so they create the illusion of continuity.

Our experience of the world is like watching a movie. On the screen we see continuity, but when we visit the projection room, what do we see? We realize that the movie is a series of still frames with little spaces or gaps between the frames. If the reel of the film moves fast enough, our eyes don't notice the gaps, the off between each frame; they only notice the on. We see a movie, and the movie is totally in our imagination. In reality, pictures are flashing in and out discontinuously on the screen.

When we're watching television and an actor appears to move from here to there, no image is actually moving across the screen. Electrons and photons are going on and off in a certain sequence. We can't see the off; we can only see the on because it's happening so fast that we create the continuity in our consciousness. Lights that seem to be moving around a Christmas tree, or a neon sign that appears to be moving, aren't really moving; they are going on and off in a certain sequence. Our perception only notices the on and not the off, so in our consciousness we create the movement of light.

The world is the vibration of the infinite, and this is how we imagine the universe into existence. Vedanta declares: "When the infinite vibrates, the worlds are born. When the infinite does not vibrate, the worlds appear to submerge. When a fiery torch is whirled fast, a circle of light appears; when it is held steady, the circle vanishes. Vibrating or not vibrating, the infinite consciousness is the same everywhere at all times. Not realizing it, one is subject to delusions; when it is realized, all delusions vanish."

Everything that we can think of — a chair, a color, a mountain, a thought, a rainbow — is just a different vibration of the same essence. Something is vibrating and creating everything, and that vibration is happening in the presence of the soul. The soul vibrates, and it creates thoughts. The soul vibrates, and it creates the body. The soul vibrates, and it creates the whole universe. Ancient people said this. Egyptian alchemists said this. So did the Greek philosophers, and so does anybody who has any idea of how creation occurs. They all say creation is a vibration.

To create is to bring into being, or existence. And to create something new, we have to die to what is. If we don't die to what is, there is no creativity. Something has to die for something new to emerge, and our soul is constantly taking quantum leaps of creativity. What is a quantum leap? It's when a subatomic particle moves from here to there without going through the space in-between. So it's here, then it's there. In between where was it? Nowhere. How did it get from here to there? Don't know. And not only did it get from here to there; it got from here to there instantly. There was no *time* for it to get from here to there. That's a quantum leap.

Every death is an opportunity for a quantum leap of creativity. Through death, we re-create ourselves at every level: the material level of the body-mind, the intellect, the personality. All of these have to die in order to re-create ourselves. With every death we store the wisdom of our experiences since the beginning of time and take quantum leaps of creativity so that we can look at ourselves again as if for the first time. Cycles of birth, transformation, and death keep us ever fresh so that we can imagine new realms for our own existence.

In biology there's a term called *apoptosis*, which means programmed cellular death. In the absence of apoptosis, cells forget to die, and this condition is called *cancer*. Cancer cells have lost the memory of death; they don't know how to die, and in their quest for immortality, they kill the host body upon which they are dependent for their life.

Death, therefore, is the ticket to life, and death is happening right now in our body-mind. Where is our two-year-old body? It's dead. The body of the two-year-old is dead, the thoughts of the two-year-old are dead, the emotions of the two-year-old are dead, the personality of the two-year-old is dead. We traded all these in for the three-year-old by dying to the two-year-old. Birth and death are happening all the time at all of these levels.

So when people ask if the soul lives on after death, the answer is yes. But does the personality survive death? In truth, the personality doesn't even survive while we are alive. The individual we think of as "me" is different from hour to hour, day to day, week to week, year to year. When we say "me," which person are we talking about — the child full of innocence and wonder, the young person full of romance and bursting with desire, or the elderly person bordering on senility? If the personality survives death, which one of these are we talking about?

The caterpillar dies to become a chrysalis. In the slumber of the chrysalis, the energies incubate and rearrange themselves, and a butterfly is born. Is the caterpillar the same being as the chrysalis or the butterfly? It is the same intelligence that has become something else. And in that something else, every cell is different, every expression of the energy in its body is different. Nothing has really died; it has only transformed.

The transformation after death is not a movement to some other place or time; it is just a change in the quality of attention in consciousness. It is a condition or state of vibrational quality of our own awareness. The world that we are experiencing with earth and sky, plants and people, sun and moon, is a particular expression of consciousness at one particular frequency. Heavens and hells and purgatories, the Earth and stars and galaxies, the elements and myriad life forms, are not locations in space-time; they are the projections of states of consciousness. These states of consciousness are vibratory expressions of the infinite consciousness, in which the cosmos moves and lives and has its existence. Infinite frequencies of consciousness coexist, and so there is the simultaneous presence of many planes of existence.

If we listen to a symphony with a one hundred–piece orchestra, all of the instruments are vibrating at different frequencies, and yet the presence of one does not displace any of the others. If our ears could hear only one frequency, we would miss out on the rest of the symphony and perhaps hear only one instrument out of the hundred. Ninety-nine percent of the music would be unavailable to us because we were not tuned in to the other frequencies.

Electromagnetic energy, which includes visible light, contains all the colors of the spectrum in the same beam of light. That same electromagnetic radiation, however, contains invisible light, such as x-rays, microwaves, radio waves, and radar. Visible and invisible light are part of the same spectrum, which is vibrating simultaneously at different frequencies. The whole spectrum coexists simultaneously, and yet we only experience what we call *visible* light.

Every pinpoint of creation contains all of these different vibrating frequencies simultaneously, and one does not displace another from its location either in space or time. With the correct instrument for tuning in to a particular frequency, we can pick out any vibration we choose. Just consider all of the instruments we use every day, such as radios, televisions, and cellular phones, to tune in to different frequencies.

At this very moment, you are surrounded by an infinity of planes; all of these vibratory realms exist right next to you. In the field of infinite possibilities, as pure potential, you exist on all of these levels simultaneously. But at the level of experience, you exist in only one — your own projected plane of existence at any one time. If you could shift your perception right now into a different vibratory frequency, you could experience another reality.

When people have near-death experiences, they have for a moment vibrated at a higher frequency and then come back to their normal vibratory frequency. Frequently, in the final moments of death, people see their whole life flash before their eyes in a split second. This is because the experience is generated through photons, which move at the speed of light. Near-death experiences confirm that every second contains the information of the whole of eternity. They also demonstrate that the journey after death is into non-locality, the domain of the soul.

During material existence, our physical body is the expression of our soul at a lower frequency, giving us the appearance of being localized in space-time. We also have an astral body that accompanies the physical body and mirrors all of its informational and energy content. In death, the physical body disintegrates, leaving the astral body as the expression of our soul at a higher frequency.

The essence of your being is a changeless reality that creates an energy pattern that comes and goes. This pattern, which is born and dies, and is constantly changing its name and shape, is the person you confuse yourself with. You may think that a personal "I am" is the cause and source of all that happens to you, but this is a hoax, a hallucination created out of a distorted perception. You must let go of the idea that you are a set personality fixed in space and time. The personality is just an illusion. What appears to be the personal "I am" is the universal "I am," the Beingness in all beings.

The real "I am" is the whole endless process of pure potentiality expressing itself in different disguises: I am pure potentiality. I am the universe. I am whatever is happening. If I look outside and see the stars and galaxies, that is what is happening, and that is me. I am the light, and I am the eyes that perceive it. I am the music, and I am the ears that hear it. I am the wind, and I am the bird's wings that fly on it. There is no other "I am" than the one Being, the entire universe.

That which you call *yourself* is constantly undergoing change and transformation. All is transforming, yet nothing ever dies. The drop of water becomes vapor, which forms a cloud that falls as rain or snow or ice. The cloud transforms into water, and the water transforms into the flowing river and the frozen lake, which melts and eventually returns to the ocean, where drops of water become vapor again.

The ocean of infinite consciousness gives birth to the billions of souls in this world. It expresses itself as the infinite diversity of life, and yet its nature remains the same. It's always there. It never disappears; it only transforms. So, too, we do not lose our soul, our true essence, as we transform into all of these molecules, all of these minds, all of these bodies, all of these relationships. Just as in life, so beyond death there is continued transformation of that which we call the individual.

As the poet Rumi said in one of his most memorable lines, "When I die, I shall soar with angels, and when I die to the angels, what I shall become you cannot imagine." And why can't we imagine this? Because when we die, we've got to be there to see what exists in the next realm of our imagination.

So what does all of this mean? It all means simply one thing: Being manifests by becoming. Birth and death, and on and off, and pleasure and pain, and night and day, and the cycles of the seasons are just the cycles of Being and becoming. This universe would be dead, it would be static, it would be rhythmless, undancing, and mummified, if it weren't for this play of *veda*, or pure knowledge, becoming *vishwa*, the universe, the eternal dance of creation. This eternal dance of creation is our essential Being, the field of pure potentiality.

When you know your true essence, you get in touch with that part of yourself that is beyond time and space and the source of both. You no longer identify with the changing *behavior* of the ocean of consciousness in all its different forms; you identify with the unchanging *essence* of consciousness itself. If you know that your essence is the unity of one spirit, then everything else becomes known to you.

Are you ready to take a quantum leap of creativity? Beyond the illusion of a material world is a world of power, freedom, and grace. Understand your true essence, and you begin a journey toward enlightenment. By and by on this journey, you shed your habitual and conditioned responses. As you do so, you become a spiritual master and transcend all suffering, including the fear of death. You realize that the real you was never born, and therefore can never die. Only that which has a beginning has an ending. That which never began is eternal and always, and it is you.

∽

Key Points

- When you die, you don't go anywhere; your soul is simply vibrating at another frequency.

- All is transforming, and yet nothing ever dies. Just as in life, so beyond death you continue to transform.

- When you identify with the eternal spirit, the unchanging essence of consciousness itself, you transcend all suffering, including the fear of death.

· 6 ·

What is the key to lasting happiness?

Source (sôrs):
One that causes, creates, or initiates; a maker.

Behind the curtain of your intellect and emotions is your self-image or ego. The ego is not your real self; it is the *image* of yourself that you have slowly built over time. It is the mask behind which you hide, but it is not the real you. And because it is not the real you, but a fraud, it lives in fear. It wants approval. It needs to control. And it follows you wherever you go.

There is a beautiful poem by the Indian poet Rabindranath Tagore, who is speaking to God: "I came out alone on my way to my tryst. But who is this that follows me in the silent dark? I move aside to avoid his presence, but I escape him not. He makes the dust rise from the earth with his swagger; he adds his loud voice to every word that I utter. He is my own little self, my Lord; he knows no shame. But I am ashamed to come to thy door in his company."

The ego is the prison you have built around yourself, and now it holds you captive within its walls. How do you know this has happened? You have to know that any time you feel discomfort in your body, your ego, which is *e-g-o* or *edging-god-out*, is overshadowing your inner self. Fear, doubt, worry, and concern are some of the energies associated with your ego.

And what do you do? The best way to dissipate these energies is to feel your body. Just feel the localized sensations in your body, and keep feeling them until they begin to dissipate. And how do you break free from captivity? You break free by choosing to identify with your inner self, the *real* you. You break free from the prison of conditioning when you feel neither beneath anyone nor superior to anyone, when you shed the need to control other people, when you create space for others to be who they are and for your real self to be what it is.

You break free when you no longer defend your point of view, when you no longer use stereotypes or harbor extreme likes or dislikes toward people you hardly know. You break free when you refuse to follow the impulses of anger and fear, when you act from humility rather than belligerence, when you tread gently rather than with a swagger, when your speech is nurturing rather than scathing, when you choose to express only your love.

And how do you know when you are free? You know you are free when you feel happy and at ease instead of fearful and anxious. You know you are free when you are independent of the good and bad opinions of others, when you have relinquished the need to seek approval, when you believe that you are good enough as you are. You know you are free when you surrender to the moment, to what is, and trust that the universe is on your side. You know you are free when you let go of resentments and grievances and choose to forgive.

A prayer in the spiritual guidebook *A Course in Miracles* says that every decision we make is a choice between a grievance and a miracle. By letting go of grievances, we choose miracles, because grievances are the melodrama of the ego that overshadows the spirit. When you relinquish all grievances, judgments, and resentments, you truly break free and find your soul.

The soul is the source of creativity, understanding, peace, harmony, laughter, and all possibilities. It is a place of stillness, which is beyond labels. But as soon as we use a label, whatever the label, we create an image that overshadows what is real. Somebody once asked Rumi, "Who are you?" And he replied, "I do not know who I am. I am in astounding lucid confusion! If you label me and define me, you will starve yourself of yourself. If you box me down with labels and definitions, that box will be your coffin. I am your own voice echoing off the walls of God!"

Rumi is saying that we create our self-image by all the labels that people give us. Without those labels, we are the free spirit and the free flow of the universe. As soon as the labels come, good or bad, then the self-image, or ego, begins to overshadow the inner self.

The world of the ego is time-bound, temporary, fragmented, fearful, personal, self-centered, self-absorbed, and attached to the known. It clings to pleasure and recoils from pain. The world of spirit is timeless and eternal, free of past and future, whole, joyful, open and accessible to all. The world of spirit is the world of community, insight, and love. This world is real, undivided, unshakable, dynamic, creative, self-sufficient, powerful, and free of limitation, expectation, and attachment.

The world of spirit is the source of all power. There never was and never will be any other source of power. What the world calls *power* is really fear that leads to manipulation and control of others, which in turn leads to violence and suffering. Real power is the power to create, the power to transform, the power to love, the power to heal, and the power to be free. Real power comes from our connection to our deepest self, to what is real. That is why powerful people are *self-referred*, not *object-referred*. These two terms need a further explanation.

As we have seen, *object-referral* means that we identify with our self-image or the objects of our experience to understand ourselves. These objects can be situations, circumstances, people, or things, but whenever we refer to objects to define our identity, we are operating out of object-referral mode. Object-referred individuals evaluate, understand, and try to know themselves through the eyes of others. The characteristic ingredients of object-referral are conditioned thinking and conditioned response, which means living under the hypnosis of social conditioning.

The first sign of object-referral is fatigue. Why? Because we have relinquished our power to the object of reference. Ultimately, this causes discomfort in our body, or even disease. Object-referral is the basic cause of unhappiness, and in the Vedic worldview, happiness is the most important factor in health.

There is an interesting fable from India that illustrates what object-referral is all about. There was once a man who had only two things that he valued in his life. One was his son, and the other was a little pony. His whole sense of reality came from referring to these two objects. Then one day the pony disappeared. The man was devastated because he had lost half of what he truly valued. He was in the depths of despair thinking about his lost pony, when the pony returned with a beautiful white stallion. Suddenly from the depths of despair he was in the heights of ecstasy.

The next day, his son was riding the stallion and fell down and broke his leg. So from the heights of ecstasy, the man was now in the depths of despair. He was wallowing in his misery when the government's army came looking for all the young men to go to war. They took every young man in the village except the man's son, because he had a broken leg. So from the depths of despair, this man was now in the heights of ecstasy. You can guess, of course, that this story of object-referral has no ending.

By their very nature objects change, and as long as we identify with objects, we will never know our real essence. When we evaluate and understand ourselves through objects, or through the eyes of others, our life is like a roller-coaster ride because the only constant about people, things, situations, and circumstances is that they change. If our identity is tied to these, then life is always going to be unstable.

The opposite of object-referral is *self-referral*. When we are self-referred, we identify with our inner self, the unchanging essence of our soul. We feel wonderful regardless of the situation, circumstance, or environment we are in. And why do we feel wonderful all the time? Because we don't identify with the situation; we are the detached, *silent witness* of the situation. We are secure in who we are, and we have no urge to prove this to anyone. If we had the urge to prove this to someone, then we would again be evaluating ourselves through the eyes of others. Self-referral is an internal state of joy, and this is different from happiness for a reason.

Of course there's always a reason to be happy. Somebody says, "I love you," and that makes you feel happy. You win the lottery and make a million dollars; that makes you feel happy. This kind of happiness is an expression of object-referral: You're happy because of this; you're happy because of that. But inner joy is independent of the situation, circumstances, people, or things. When you experience inner joy, you are happy for no reason. Just the mere fact of being alive to gaze at the stars, to experience the beauty of this world, to be experientially alive in the miracle of life itself is your happiness.

Everything in life is transient and changing because that is the nature of our world. But when you are self-referred, you enjoy the change instead of resisting it. People have asked me, "What about situations that are difficult to accept? If something bad is happening in my life, how can I be happy instead of negative and depressed?" Well, by going back to your source, by recognizing that whatever is happening, it comes and goes. You don't need to look positively or negatively at a difficult situation. To always look positively at a difficult situation is artificial, isn't it? If I were positive all the time, first of all I'd be terribly boring. Second, I'd be terribly unnatural. Third, nobody would want to be with me. To always look negatively at a difficult situation is also unnatural. I'd just become exasperatingly negative and a total bore. To be natural is the best state to be.

I once had a patient with a serious disease, and I had never seen her in a mood that was not so-called positive. She was exasperatingly positive, and finally I had to ask her how she could do that. She broke down and said she was petrified of having a negative thought. But isn't being petrified of having a negative thought a negative thought in itself? Of course it is, so we don't need to manipulate our thinking. To manipulate our thinking is an artificial thing, and one which the Vedic tradition calls *mood making*.

It's better to be spontaneous, and in the spontaneity is joyfulness. It's better to be natural, and to let the universe play itself out through us.

What is a negative mind? It's an interpretation. What is a positive mind? It's also an interpretation. And the difference between a positive mind and a negative mind is sometimes quite superficial. If you ask me if it's preferable to have a positive mind, I'd say, "Of course. A positive mind is preferable to a negative mind," but both a positive mind and a negative mind can be a turbulent mind, and sometimes one can switch to the other very quickly. Courage can become fear in the twinkling of an eye. Love can transform into jealousy in the twinkling of an eye. These are turbulent minds. More important than a positive mind is a silent mind.

We have to learn to go beyond both a positive mind and a negative mind to become a silent, nonjudgmental, nonanalytical, noninterpretive mind. In other words, the silent witness. In the process of silent witnessing, we experience inner silence. In the purity of silence, we feel connected to our source and to everything else. The tendencies that emerge from this connection are evolutionary and spontaneous. In silence, we just flow with the tide and spontaneously become nonjudgmental, nonanalytical, and noninterpretive about situations, circumstances, other people, and ourselves. In silence, inner energies spontaneously wake up and bring about the appropriate transformation for every situation.

There's a saying that goes, "The river of life runs between the banks of pleasure and pain, and one bumps into both." That's not the problem. The problem occurs when we cling to the banks, either the positive one or the negative one. When we quietly reconcile ourselves to all the contradictions that life offers, when we can comfortably flow between the banks of pleasure and pain, experiencing them both while getting stuck in neither, then we have achieved freedom.

Joy and sorrow, happiness and suffering, are the play of opposites; they are transient because they are time-bound. Spirit, the essential you, is independent of the play of opposites; it dwells in the silent bliss of the eternal. And when you know yourself as this field of pure consciousness, then you are living from the source, which *is* bliss.

That's why the key to lasting happiness is to stop looking for it, and to know that you already have it. If you look for happiness, you will never find it. If you think it's around the corner, then you will keep turning corners. The real key to happiness is to live and play in the field of intelligence that is beyond positive and negative. That field is your source, and it is magical, holy, joyful, and free.

Happiness and sadness are different faces of infinite consciousness. Both are transient, and you are neither because you are not a state of consciousness. You are consciousness itself expressing all of these states. Why would you want to identify with a wave on the ocean or a mere drop of water when you are the ocean? You are not the ever-changing *behavior* of the ocean. You are the *water-i-ness* of the ocean. And this water-i-ness doesn't change.

The real nature of a person is Being, which is not thought. To experience lasting happiness, you have to go to a place beyond thought and experience inner peace. It's not that you have to have a positive attitude. It's not that you have to shed your sadness and bring in happiness. You have to go beyond both; otherwise, it's just another version of positive thinking. You have to go beyond the world of duality to the field of pure potentiality and live from your source.

Rumi, in one of his eloquent poems says, "Out beyond ideas of right-doing and wrong-doing, there is a field. I'll meet you there." This field is not in the realm of thought. It's beyond all concepts, ideas, and interpretations. In this field that Rumi is talking about, there is power to manifest your desires, there is freedom from fear and limitations, and there is that good-luck factor known as grace, which is the fulfillment of desire through synchronicity and the support of the laws of nature.

But first you have to go beyond duality, beyond the labels of good and bad, right and wrong. Just as truth, goodness, harmony, and beauty are the sponta-neous evolutionary impulses of the universe, so, too, are evil, inertia, chaos, confusion, and destruction the spontaneous evolutionary impulses of the universe. And it's the tension between the two that makes life meaningful. What would life be if there wasn't this contrast? Life would be dull. Have you ever been to a movie where everything is always fine? It's boring!

The whole of creation is contrast, tension, divine discontent. If there were only truth, goodness, har-mony, and beauty, the universe would expand and dis-appear. There has to be something to hold it back. If there were only the destructive inertial forces, then the universe would rapidly burn itself up into the heat death of absolute zero. It would collapse into a black hole — *ssshveet!* — and disappear. So there's both. There's the *play* between both; otherwise this world would not exist.

All experience in life is by contrast because the universe creates through contrast: light and dark, pleasure and pain, birth and death, hot and cold. If there were no contrast, there would be no experience. There is pleasure because there is pain, there is joy because there is sorrow, there is hot because there is cold, there is wealth because there is poverty, there is courage because there is fear, and there is love because there is the opposite of love. Unless we know both, one is meaningless and cannot be experienced. There is a saying in India: "A blind man from birth cannot know what darkness is because he has never experienced light."

The mind is made up of opposing energies that spark and create the fire of life. Inside us is both the divine and the diabolical, the sinner and the saint, the sacred and the profane. Inside us is forbidden lust and unconditional love, the beatitude of paradise, and the dark night of the soul. We are all of these things because we are a field of all possibilities. Just imagine a world of Pollyannas. Would you *really* want to be in that world?

When we're standing in the light, then we have a shadow. If we don't have a shadow, then we're standing in darkness. The shadow is the part of us that we're ashamed of, that we don't want people to know about. It's that part of us that we hide away in the closet. The shadow is dark, it's secretive, it's primitive, it's shrouded in mythology. And if we ignore the shadow, it tends to say, *Well, I'm going to embarrass you. I want you to notice me.*

When you exhibit so-called positive and negative qualities, you are not flawed; you are complete. When you are comfortable with your shadow, when you embrace your shadow because this is how the infinite consciousness made you, then you are attractive beyond measure, and your life is an adventure. You are natural when you are comfortable with your ambiguity, and nothing is more beautiful than being natural. When you are comfortable with both your strengths and weaknesses, you radiate simple, unaffected humanity. This is the essence of being lovable because you are not subject to behaviors that drive love away. You do not constantly look for approval by getting caught up in thinking, *What do others think of me? Am I superior, am I inferior? Do people like me, or do they dislike me?*

You don't constantly compare yourself to an ideal that doesn't exist. Your ego doesn't say to you, *I'm not good enough. I'm not pretty enough. I'm not handsome enough. I'm not rich enough.*

If your experience of yourself is object-referred, it is fear-based and resistant to what is. If your experience of yourself is self-referred, it is love-based and accepting of what is. Self-referred people are natural and unaffected by the opinions of others. They are innocent, simple, and childlike: *Thank you, God, for making me just like I am. I have good things, and I have bad things; I have all things in me. I am complete.* Self-acceptance, *total* self-acceptance, means self-forgiveness. When you forgive yourself and stop judging yourself, then you won't judge others, and there will be less conflict in the world.

All relationship is a mirror to the self. Those whom you are deeply attracted to or repelled by are both mirrors of you. You are attracted to those in whom you find traits that you already have but want more of, and you are repelled by those in whom you find traits that you deny in yourself. Identify the qualities that attract you to others, and the qualities that repel you. Write them down on a piece of paper. This is who you are. And if you accept yourself as you are, and love yourself as you are, you become immensely attractive because you are natural.

Why not make yourself irresistible? Embrace your shadow, understand your shadow, forgive your shadow. Embrace the fact that you are the many faces of the divine: You are the prisoner, and you are the prison; you are the jailor, and you are the freedom also. It is your destiny to play an infinity of roles, but you are not the roles you play.

Right now I'm playing the role of an author. When I think of my children, I'm playing the role of a father. When I think of my wife, I'm playing the role of a husband. When I think of my parents, I'm playing the role of a child. When I think of a patient, I'm playing the role of a doctor. But I am none of these roles that I play. I am the eternal spirit, the silent witness who plays these roles.

In the great chain of being, where birth and death are the opening and closing of acts in the eternal drama of existence, we have all played an infinity of roles for ages beyond our imagination. Even after death, our spirit will continue to play other roles. To be independent of the roles we play, and yet to play the roles with passion, is detached involvement. As we will see in Chapter 8, this happens naturally when we abide in cosmic consciousness. We are involved and yet we are free at the same time. In cosmic consciousness, the whole process of life begins to blossom effortlessly. We experience more joy, greater ease, and the state of grace because we allow universal intelligence to play itself through us.

Whatever is happening around you is transient. If it's joy and pleasure, you can be sure there's a bit of the opposite around the corner. If it's suffering and misery, you can be sure there's a bit of the opposite around the corner, too. But in cosmic consciousness you are independent of the play of opposites; you are independent of both hope and despair. Hope is nothing but a sign of despair. When you say, "I have hope," you are implying that you are in despair. You have to go beyond hope and despair, and you can only do that if you ground yourself in the wisdom of who you really are — not just intellectually but experientially.

Anything and everything in existence can be mastered when you experience the truth of who you are. Once your mind is absorbed in the unbounded nature of pure consciousness, you are no longer upset by the play of opposites. You witness the world of duality, but you live in the field of pure potentiality. This is living from the source of lasting happiness — the source of power, freedom, and grace.

∽

Key Points

- The key to lasting happiness is to identify with the unchanging essence of your inner self, your source. Then you no longer look for happiness because you know that you already have it.

- More important than a positive mind is a silent mind. A silent mind is a nonjudgmental, nonanalytical, noninterpretive mind.

- When you can accept all the contradictions that life offers, when you can comfortably flow between the banks of pleasure and pain, experiencing both while getting stuck in neither, you have achieved freedom.

· 7 ·

How can I live with effortless ease?

*Flow (flō): To move easily and gracefully
with unbroken continuity; to hang loose.*

When you are conceived, all you are is a double strand of DNA — a speck of information and intelligence that differentiates into a hundred trillion cells, which then become a fully formed baby with eyes, nose, ears, brain, arms, legs, genitals. You didn't do anything to make that happen, and yet you made it happen. In that blueprint, that speck of information, is a plan for when your teeth will grow out, when you will reach puberty, when you will generate sex hormones so you can produce another human being. It's all there in the speck, and it happens with effortless spontaneity, with effortless ease, with no resistance. The impulse of the universe is coming through you in the form of that double strand of DNA.

Now, if you can make a hundred trillion cells without any confusion, if each cell can do its own unique thing and correlate its activity with every other cell without any confusion, it's because the intelligence of the universe is flowing through that speck of DNA, which you can't even see under a microscope. So the best thing you can do is to allow it to happen. It isn't wise to interfere with it.

And how do you interfere with this intelligence? In spiritual terms, we can say that you interfere when you identify with your self-image and lose your inner self; when you lose your sense of connection with your soul, your source. In more common terms, we can say that you interfere when you start worrying, when you start anticipating problems, when you start thinking,

What can go wrong? When you try to control everything, when you are afraid, when you feel isolated —
all these things interfere with the flow of nature's
intelligence.

Your inner self is your innate intelligence; it is
Being becoming. It is your ability to create, to grow, to
evolve, to express. Your self-image is the indoctrination
by society, by education; it's the image you have created
of yourself based on what other people think of you.
As soon as you sacrifice the Self for the self-image,
you lose divinity for something that is illusory and
doesn't exist. The self-image is a hallucination; it isn't
even real, but it interferes with the flow of intelligence.

Innate intelligence is spontaneous, intuitive, evolutionary, and whole. It is the flow of the whole universe acting through you. But fear, doubt, concern,
and worry put you in a contracted state that interferes
with the spontaneous flow of intelligence. What we
call *stress* is that which actually constricts the flow
of intelligence as it moves from the unmanifest to
the manifest.

Anytime you feel resistance, anytime things are going wrong, anytime you feel frustration, anytime there is too much effort, then you are not connecting with your source, the field of pure potentiality. The state of fear is the state of separation; it is resistance to what is. If you don't have resistance, then it's all spontaneous, effortless ease.

The mind, being everywhere, is nonlocal, and through the process of attention we localize it. So if we want something to become our life experience, then we put our attention on it. If we don't want something to become our life experience, we take our attention away from it. In fact, the whole mechanics of creation is just that: a certain quality of attention of the Self to itself.

Right now, you're probably not aware that your foot is touching the sole of your shoe or that your naked skin is touching your clothes. As soon as you put your attention on this fact, it becomes your reality. The basic principle is this: Whatever you put your attention on grows stronger in your life.

When people experience pain, they try to avoid it or they want to escape from it. And the more they try to do that, the more their attention is on the *idea* of pain. The idea of pain gets magnified, and of course that creates more pain. So if you have a headache and you want to get rid of it, then simply be with the headache; be with the pain. Don't analyze, don't interpret, and don't try to judge the pain. Feel the sensation with your full awareness. Put your attention on the sensation, and you'll see that it dissipates. Pure consciousness is a healing force, so when you put your attention on the sensation, consciousness gets into it and saturates it with the healing force of life. If, however, you put your attention on the *idea* of pain, then the pain will become more pronounced.

When you go beyond thought, beyond the *idea* of pain, then you are Being. And when you are Being, you are not thinking. From that level of awareness, you simply put your attention on the body as a witness, not thinking this or that notion, just being aware. Anything you can *think* of is a notion. Pain is a notion;

suffering is a notion; happiness is a notion; time is a notion; wealth is a notion; poverty is a notion. There is nothing that exists that was not a notion first, or an idea, or a concept, or some form of desire. But the *source* of the thought, the *thinker* behind the thought, is not a notion. It is pure Being, pure potentiality.

What does Being do in order to manifest as matter? It has an idea, it has a notion, and that notion immediately localizes the field of all possibilities into this or that reality. The scriptures say, "In the beginning there was the word, and the word was made into flesh, and the word was with God." This is the exact mechanics of manifestation. What is the word? The word is an idea, it's a notion, it's a concept, and that concept is the spontaneous manifestation of an impulse in consciousness. That's all it is.

Being is not a concept because Being is nonconceptualizable; it is beyond all concepts. Being has no beginning in time, no ending in time, no edges in space. We are really being humans instead of human beings. We have found the mode of expression to be human, but essentially we are pure Being. This may seem like an abstract notion, but if you go beyond thought and experience Being, you will realize that it isn't.

Most people get attached to concepts and notions rather than the experience of Being. This is analogous to mistaking the map for the territory. The territory is the experience of Being, and it's the reality that we want to experience. The map is just the labeling of a territory, and yet we mostly identify with the map. What we have to understand once and for all is that we are not the thought, but the one who generates the thought.

Being is the source of thought, and it's also where fulfillment of desire comes from. What is desire? Desire is pure potentiality seeking manifestation. But fulfillment of desire requires that we first Be, and then simply having the notion in our awareness spontaneously creates the reality. This is the mechanics of creation; it's how the universe comes into being. The universe is a field of all possibilities that interacts with its own self. Therefore, inherent in every desire is the mechanics for the spontaneous fulfillment of the desire. All that is required is attention and noninterference.

When I have the desire to walk from here to there, my body does it. I don't fully verbalize the instructions for my body to move from here to there; it happens spontaneously. When I go to sleep at night, I don't lie down in the bed and say, *Come on, body, change your state of consciousness to the sleep state.* I don't *try* to go to sleep. Inherent in having the desire is the mechanics for the transformation of my physiology to go to sleep. In fact, anything that happens in my body is a faint desire, and the less I worry about the mechanics of it, the more efficient it is. The moment I start worrying about the mechanics of it, it loses its efficiency and interferes with the flow of innate intelligence.

No matter what the desire, we don't want to interfere with it. To interfere means to produce an unwanted result, and the way we interfere with the manifestation of desire is by trying too hard, by using too much effort. We interfere when we doubt, when we listen to others' opinions, when we get lost in our attachment to the result, instead of just being and having the notion, the desire.

If you watch a ballplayer hit a ball, and a fielder go after the catch, do they worry about the mechanics of the sport? No, their actions are completely spontaneous. Even before the batter has hit the ball, the fielder has started moving, intending nonverbally in awareness the mechanics of going after the ball. The game plays itself out through the athletes. Once desire begins to flow, thought is not involved at all; everything is completely nonverbal. The players simply move spontaneously and effortlessly in the right direction. This is the key to fulfilling any desire, and it's also the key to efficient action.

The universe expresses itself through effortless Being. It is pure potentiality seeking manifestation by having the desire and just letting go. Good musicians will tell you that peak experiences come when they don't seem to be playing the music; the music is playing itself out through them. Accomplished dancers will tell you that after a while it doesn't feel like they are doing the dance; the dance is expressing itself through the dancer. This is how inspired poets write poems or lyricists write lyrics; the words just come to them. This is magical thinking, and once you've had a little taste of it, it's enough to change your whole life.

When gardeners plant seeds, they don't try to make them sprout, they don't doubt that the seeds will grow into plants. Other people's opinions do not interfere with their conviction that within each seed is everything necessary to create a plant. And gardeners don't get lost in their attachment to the result; they know the result is there. So to use our power effectively when it comes to our own desires, we have to relinquish our attachment to the outcome. But this doesn't mean that we don't want the outcome. Of course we prefer the outcome to anything else, but we are not rigidly *attached* to it.

Attachment is a form of fear, doubt, and worry, and this constricts the flow of nature's intelligence. When we have a desire, we know what our intention is, and we just let go, trusting the universe to organize all the details for its manifestation. There's no concern about the outcome; we just release our desire from our heart, and let it flow through us with the impulse of the universe. The more we detach and let go, the more spontaneously our desires are fulfilled.

The old belief in suffering says, *I have to work hard to accomplish my goals, and the harder I work, the more likely it is that my goals will get accomplished.* This is a very Western concept, but does nature work like that? Do you see any effort in the migration of a bird from Siberia to South America? Do you see any effort in the ability of the body-mind's intelligence to orchestrate an infinite number of things while monitoring the movement of the entire cosmos? Do you see any effort in a seed becoming a tree and bearing fruit?

Nature functions with maximum efficiency, and this principle in nature is *do less, accomplish more.* This is the law of least effort. If we mirror the way nature works, we can also do less and accomplish more. We can go to that field of silence from where all creativity comes; we can have a desire, let go, and watch the results as they come. And when things don't seem to go our way, we let go of our idea of how things should be, trusting that for the moment at least, we do not know the larger picture. In the overall context, that larger picture is good for us. We understand that our life has a purpose that fits into the overall purpose of the cosmos. Our attitude, therefore, is one of detachment and acceptance because we know that the universe is on our side.

The universe is handling all the details for everything and everybody else, and we know that it is doing so for us. We have complete confidence in universal intelligence to take care of all the details. This intelligence is, after all, managing all the details of our body-mind. This intelligence is managing all the details of the natural world; it's keeping the stars and planets in their position. If we can trust it to do all of that, then we can trust it to handle the details of our desire. Trust in nature's infinite organizing power is an important component of the state of grace. To live in grace is to live with ease and lack of struggle because we trust that nature's intelligence is flowing through us. We don't interfere.

Remember, gardeners plant seeds and then let go. They give their garden attention — their *unconditional* attention — and they have no doubt. It's the same thing for you. Have a goal in your awareness, give it your attention, and have no doubt. Be effortless about it, and the desire will manifest. Desires are like seeds left in the ground. They wait for the right season, and then spontaneously bloom into beautiful flowers and majestic trees.

∽

KEY POINTS

- You can live with effortless ease by allowing universal intelligence to flow through you without interference in the form of fear, resistance, or attachment.

- Inherent in every desire is the mechanics for its spontaneous fulfillment. Desire is pure potentiality seeking manifestation.

- When you are stressed, when you anticipate problems, when you use too much effort, you constrict the flow of nature's intelligence as it moves from the unmanifest to the manifest.

· 8 ·

When will I be fully awake?

Whole · ness (hōl' nĭs): Containing all the elements;
complete in itself; not divided; unity.

Some people believe that our relationships, our
environment, and the situations and circumstances
around us create our state of mind. Others have pro-
claimed that it's the other way around — that our
state of mind creates our relationships, our environment, and the situations and circumstances of our life.
Neither of these perspectives is true. Both our inner
world and our outer world interdependently co-arise,

depending on the level of vibration of our spirit. They form a feedback loop that continues to perpetuate itself unless we move to a different vibrational quality of awareness. Both the world around us and our state of mind are expressions of where we are in our evolution at this moment.

Every day we normally experience three states of consciousness: waking, dreaming, and sleeping. But only by spending time in silence, stillness, or meditation do we experience a fourth state of consciousness where we start to glimpse our soul. When we glimpse our soul, we become a little more intuitive. We start to feel that things are not just what they seem to be; there is something more behind the scenes.

The physical world we normally experience is a shadow of the real world. The real world, the world of spirit, exists behind a veil, and the veil is our own conditioning. In truth, we are not bound by the world of space, time, matter, and causation, but the veil prevents us from seeing this truth. It also prevents us from living in power, freedom, and grace.

In the fourth state of consciousness, we begin to sense the deeper reality that is orchestrating the physical world, and there is a tearing in the veil that separates the physical and spiritual realms. Just as we have to wake up from the dream state to experience waking consciousness, we have to wake up from what we call *waking consciousness* to glimpse our spirit, our inner self. This is called *glimpsing the soul,* and it's the fourth state of consciousness. It's simply to be in touch with our soul.

This leads to a fifth state of consciousness, or *cosmic consciousness,* when our soul fully wakes up in waking, dreaming, and sleeping. Our body can be fast asleep, but our soul, the silent witness, is watching the body in deep sleep. Our body can be walking, and the silent witness is watching the body walk. Our body can be playing tennis, and the silent witness is watching the body play tennis. Our awareness is localized in space-time, and it's nonlocal, or transcendent, at the same time.

Just as Christ said, "I am in this world, but not of it," in cosmic consciousness we are still in this world

— waking, dreaming, and sleeping — and yet we are connected to our source in waking, dreaming, and sleeping. Like a lamp at the door that shines inside the room and outside the room, we are in both places. When this happens, synchronicity, chance encounters, and hidden clues increase. We start to understand the power of intention. We start to watch our internal dialogue, and we say, *I know that how I speak to myself actually causes things to change in my physiology, in my world.*

In cosmic consciousness, we find that relationship is the most important thing in life; everything in life is a confluence of relationships. We begin to see that everything is a balance between feminine and masculine energies, the yin and yang, and anytime there is more of one than the other, we are out of balance. Right now, we need to reawaken the feminine because the dominance of the masculine has led to belligerence, arrogance, and aggression, the very problems we see in the world right now.

In cosmic consciousness, we are aware that we are not the physical body, nor are we the mind and all the roles we play. We are the silent witness, and a sense of freedom and liberation comes out of this awareness. We are involved in our roles, and yet we are free at the same time. Then we recognize that after death our spirit will continue to play other roles, and we feel more ease. As we abide in cosmic consciousness and allow it to blossom, the universe plays itself through us, and the whole dance of life becomes effortless.

Once we have glimpsed our soul, we find the outside reality much more interesting because we glimpse the soul of other beings, too. We glimpse the soul of a flower, of a tree, of a mountain, of a river, and we commune with it and say, "This is my extended body. I have a personal body and I have an extended body, and they are both equally mine. Those trees are not just trees; they are my lungs. Those rivers are not just rivers; they are my circulation. This earth is my body, this air is my breath, and the fire in my heart is the fire in the stars."

If we don't interfere with nature's intelligence, then we start to awaken into the sixth state of consciousness, or *divine consciousness*. In cosmic consciousness, the spirit was fully awake in the observer in waking, dreaming, and sleeping, but now the spirit begins to awaken in that which is observed. In divine consciousness, we see and feel the presence of spirit in everything. If I look at a leaf, I say, "This is a leaf, but it's also sunshine, and earth, and water, and air, and the infinite void, and the whole universe playing the part of a leaf." The leaf is a pattern of behavior of the whole universe. The pattern is transient, it's changing, and just for the moment, spirit is localizing as a leaf.

If I take a picture of a giant wave on the ocean, the movement of the ocean is frozen by taking the picture. I show you the picture and you say, "Oh, that's a beautiful wave; let's go see it." We go to the ocean, and that wave is no longer there because what we saw in the picture was a frozen moment of observation. So, too, in the act of perception, we freeze the movement of the universe into a leaf, or a table, or a cloud, or a rainbow.

When we wake up to divine consciousness, we don't just see a leaf, or a table, or a cloud, or a rainbow;

we see the whole universe being all these things. We feel the presence of spirit naturally unfolding in whatever we observe. We're not doing anything to make this happen; we're just allowing the universe to unfold and play itself out through us.

In ordinary awareness, we see the obvious, the apparent, that which everybody else sees. But in this extraordinary awareness, we pierce the mask of appearances and go beyond to that field of light where spirit shines, where everything connects with everything else. This going beyond is a new quality of awareness. We are like a speck of awareness in the vast expanse of awareness, and our own awareness expands until it is outside the edges of space, and beyond the corridors of time.

When we enter this reality, we feel safe even in the midst of danger. No matter how turbulent and chaotic the world is around us, we feel deep peace inside ourselves. In the noise and din of everyday existence, in the marketplace of life where everyone haggles, we feel an unshakable inner silence. An inner voice speaks to us, and it guides us to make spontaneous and correct choices, weaving the web of our destiny. Prayers get answered and miracles occur, and we feel wonder at the sheer fact of our existence.

In divine consciousness, the soul wakes up in everything we observe, and this awareness allows us to commune with other souls. Communion is not mere communication; it is soul making contact with soul. It is the sharing of spirit. In communion, we feel equal to all beings; we feel neither superior nor inferior to anything. In communion, we have empathy for all beings; we feel how they feel, and we communicate without the use of words.

Through communion we experience intimacy with the world. We feel the presence of spirit in ourselves and in everything, and with this shift in our consciousness, we can become what we perceive. We can commune with the spirit of anything in the natural world, and it responds to us. We can ask the cloud to rain or the tree to bear fruit, and we can perform miracles. All miracles are examples of divine consciousness, which means that the divine spirit is no longer difficult to find; the divine spirit is impossible to avoid.

Next, we awaken to the seventh state of consciousness, which is *unity consciousness*. This is when the spirit inside us, which is now fully awake, merges with the spirit inside objects, which are also now fully awake. They become one, and there is only one spirit. We are that one spirit, and the whole universe is the manifestation of that one spirit. In unity consciousness, love radiates from our heart like light from a bonfire. Our personal self becomes the universal Self, and we see the whole universe in our being.

This is when we can really understand the Vedic expression "I am not in the world; the world is in me. I am not in the body; the body is in me. I am not in the mind; the mind is in me. Body, mind, and world happen to me as I curve back within myself and create them."

Normally, we think of ourselves as a person who exists in a place, in a city, in a country, in the world. But this is not the true reality; it's the other way around.

The world exists in us. What we call *the physical body* and *the physical world* are projections of our consciousness. Without us — the "I am" — the world would not exist. John Wheeler, a theoretical physicist and colleague of Albert Einstein's, said the universe doesn't exist unless there's a conscious observer. The conscious observer could be a mosquito, or it could be me or you. But just as you can't have an electrical current unless there's a positive and negative terminal, so, too, you can't have a physical universe unless there's a creator and somebody to observe the creation.

The universe is conscious, and because it is conscious, it is conscious of itself. So infinite consciousness is its own observer. Where is the observer? The observer is in the discontinuity, the gap, the off. What is the observer observing? It has to observe itself. Before infinite consciousness observes itself, there is neither space, nor time, nor matter. Nor is there causality. There is only a possibility or potential for all these. But when the observer, which is in the discontinuity, observes itself, which is also in the discontinuity, the off observes the off and mysteriously switches on. This is how infinite consciousness interacting with itself creates the observer, the process of observation, and that which is observed. All creation is self-interaction.

Interacting with itself, infinite consciousness first creates the mind, then it creates the body, then it creates the physical world. Everything we call *physical* is a translation of different vibratory frequencies of consciousness in the mind. And the mind, in turn, is an interpretation of consciousness unto itself.

In a beautiful verse, Rumi says, "I have lived on the lip of insanity, wanting to know reasons, knocking on a door. The door opens. I've been knocking from the inside!" In other words, we are all contained in the one mind, whether we want to call it *God's mind, infinite consciousness, spirit,* or *the unified field.* There is no inside, there is no outside; it's all one activity of a single consciousness. Our fundamental nature is pure consciousness. And the soul, as an aspect of pure consciousness, has to observe pure consciousness to create space, time, matter, and causality.

In the relative, I am the observer looking at objects. In the absolute, I am the simultaneous manifestation of both the observer and the object of perception; they interdependently co-arise. At the deepest level of existence, when I look at you, I am looking at myself. My deeper self is interacting with itself and creating both me and you. When I look at a tree, I am looking at myself. My deeper self is interacting with itself to create both the observer of the tree and the tree.

The world exists in us; we do not exist in the world. This is a difficult concept, and you could spend a whole lifetime trying to understand it intellectually. However, from a practical point of view, the next time you look at a tree, or you look at another being, or you look at anything, just say to yourself, *That tree exists in me. That being exists in me. Those stars and galaxies, this table and chair — everything exists in me.* If we tell ourselves this, then soon we find ourselves having a knowingness about it. If I tell myself, *That tree exists in me,* then I'll be in love with the tree. If I tell myself that you exist in me, then

I'll be in love with you. Then sooner or later, I'll have that intimate relationship with everything in existence.

Everything in the universe is alive. The Earth, the stars, the Milky Way, and other galactic systems are a living organism. The universe is one gigantic, living Being. When we have a feeling of intimacy with this Being, when we fall in love with everything that exists, the universe speaks to us and reveals its inner-most secrets.

What we call *the laws of nature* are actually the thoughts of a sentient Being. What we call *the universe and galactic systems* are the body of that sentient Being. An electrical storm in the atmosphere of the Earth is the same electrical storm in a synaptic network of our brain. In our brain it comes as a thought; out there it comes as a flash of lightning in the sky. Is the storm in the synaptic network of our brain any different from the storm out there? As far as the universe is concerned, they are both its behavior. It's our misper-ception that makes us think, *This is me, and everything else is separate from me.*

You and I are part of a conscious universe. The universe is thinking. It's creative. It imagines. The universe is full of creativity, and it couldn't be full of creativity if it wasn't conscious. I am creative because the universe is creative. I am conscious because the universe is conscious. I think because the universe thinks. I am imbued with subjectivity because the universe is imbued with subjectivity, which means the universe has a sense of "I am. I exist." And my sense of "I am," my sense of my existence, is not separate from the universal sense of "I am."

If you could really understand this, then you would realize that you are not a solid body that exists in space and time. The essence of your being is the source of space and time. Your soul co-creates with the source of all creation. As you wake up to this awareness, you realize there is nothing you cannot create. Then one day, the consciousness that seems to be "inside" you, merges with the consciousness that seems to be "outside" you, and you see the whole universe as your own manifestation.

There is no difference between what is happening in your inner world and what is happening in your outer world. The outer world is just a reflection of your inner world. The world is a mirror of your mind, and your mind is a mirror of the world. But you are neither your mind nor the world; you are the creator of both. Even that idea is only a partial truth because there are no inner and outer worlds. There is only the self-interaction of the one Being, infinite consciousness.

This is the mystery of creation. Whatever we think within ourselves, we become in space and time, and that alone is experienced. When we are suffering and agitated, the night becomes an epoch, while a night of revelry passes by like a moment. Both the suffering and the revelry are part of the dream, and in the dream, a moment is no different from an epoch.

Vedanta declares, "Whatever is in the mind is like a city in the clouds. The emergence of this world is no more than thoughts manifesting themselves. All these worlds are no more than modifications of consciousness, and in the infinite consciousness, we have created each other."

Once we understand that there are different states of consciousness, we also come to realize that the laws of nature only apply to a waking state of consciousness, or a dream state of consciousness, or a sleeping state of consciousness in the ordinary cycles of life and activity. As we navigate in these states of consciousness, we navigate in different worlds.

The soul abides in many states of consciousness simultaneously, but what we experience each day depends on where we put our attention. Through attention, every thought, every desire, becomes a little seed of information localizing from our nonlocal soul. And because human beings are storytellers, we tell ourselves stories about our own thoughts. If we call a friend and she doesn't return our call, we may think, *She doesn't like me; maybe my nose is too long.* We tell ourselves a story, then we live out that story and we call it *a life.* The same thing happens to us at night, but the logical mind is asleep, and we call it *a dream.*

One night I dreamed that I was playing golf and won a trophy. There were a hundred people in the gallery, and they all cheered when I got this beautiful trophy. The next day my photo was in the newspaper. Then I woke up and said, "Oh my God, I made up the whole thing. I was Deepak who won the trophy. I was the golf course, I was the hundred people, and I was the photo in the newspaper." But I didn't know that when I was dreaming; I only knew it when I woke up.

Then one day I wake up from waking consciousness and realize that everything is a projection of my own consciousness, of my own inner self. In all these states of consciousness, I am the producer, the director, the actor. I am the protagonist, the hero, the villain. I am the prisoner, the guard, the prison. I am the freedom, too. And I didn't know it, but now that I'm fully awake, I know it. Now I can choose to play, and that play is called *leela*, the play of the universe.

In my native country of India, *leela* is the cosmic dance of Shiva and Shakti, the masculine and feminine powers of creation. The cosmic dance is a lovely

symbol for creation. One foot on the ground represents the stillness of the field of the absolute, and one
foot raised in a dance step represents the dynamic field
of the relative. But beyond the pretty imagery, *leela* is
about the delight and freedom of creation.

Infinite consciousness creates and plays through
us in different frequencies: deep sleep, wake up from
that into dreams, wake up from that into waking state,
wake up from that into glimpsing the soul, wake up
from that into cosmic consciousness, wake up from
that into divine consciousness, wake up from that into
unity consciousness.

Infinite consciousness is a field of all possibilities, and when the universe is flowing through us
without interference, we find all of these realities
where consciousness plays itself out as space, time,
matter, and causality. But go beyond the field of
thought, the field of emotions, the field of ego, the
field of personality, and there's only one field left.
That's who we are: the field of pure consciousness
localizing as a person.

As a person, I appear to be separate from others, so I think, *I am Deepak. I am here, and you are there. This one is a friend; that one is an enemy. This one is good; that one is bad.* But it's all a projection of consciousness. There's no such thing as "a person." What we call *a person* is infinite consciousness manifesting as a transient pattern of behavior. If you think of yourself as a person, then you will see people everywhere. But if you realize you're not a person, then you will feel the presence of spirit, the one Being, everywhere. The Being who's looking out of my eyes, and the Being who's looking out of your eyes, is the same Being in a different disguise.

The universe is the dream of the infinite consciousness, and in this dream is born the ego-sense and the fantasy that there are others. But all these others are nothing but dream objects. In the tangled hierarchy of creation, everything is inseparably one, and there is only interdependent co-creation.

Look at any object in your surroundings, perhaps a table and chair. They appear as objects in the field of your perception, but that is the superstition of materialism, the mistake of the intellect. If you rely on sensory perception alone, you will never experience the whole. You will only experience bits and pieces of reality because your eyes, and ears, and nose, and mouth, and hands are bits and pieces of sensory apparatus.

The table upon which you write, the chair upon which you sit — everything in existence, animate or inanimate — is the whole universe in a particular pattern of behavior. Go beyond the pattern of behavior, and feel the presence of that which is doing the behaving. You will see and feel the presence of spirit in every object of your perception.

The table and chair are made of wood, and every grain of the wood contains the entire history of the universe. The wood comes from trees and forests. The trees and the forests are made of sunlight and rainfall, earth and air, and the infinite void beyond the deep of space and the dark of time. The trees and the forests are inseparable from the squirrels and the birds' nests, and the whole web of life in the great chain of being. The table and chair are inseparable from the entire universe and all that it contains. They are the carpenters and factories, the employers and employees, the retailers and customers. They are all of these people and their lives and their loves, their hopes and their despair, their anguish and their pleasure, their joy and their pain.

Now you are not perceiving bits and pieces anymore; you are *seeing*. When you are fully awake, you open your eyes and really *see*. And what do you see? You see the whole in every part. The whole universe is in every part of the universe. You see the ocean in a drop of water, and perceiving that which is whole, your vision is holy. When your vision is holy, you are healed.

To heal is to return to the memory of wholeness or holiness. There is an ancient saying from India: "All this struggling to learn, when all you have to do is remember." And what do you have to remember? Your true nature.

Once you discover your real identity, you are healed on every level, and your transformation begins. A Zen poem says, "Autumn leaves, snow in winter, summer breezes, spring flowers. If you are fully awake, this is the best season in your life."

∽

KEY POINTS

- You are fully awake when you see and feel the presence of spirit in everything.

- The universe flows through you and plays through you in many different frequencies simultaneously.

- When you remember your true nature, you return to the memory of wholeness, and you are healed.

Part III

❧

The Practice

Experiencing who we are

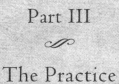

· 9 ·

What is power and how do I obtain it?

Pow · er (pou' ər):
The ability to create, to accomplish, to act effectively.

Power is the ability to manifest anything you want, including any reality that you want to experience. Real power comes from the essence of infinity, which is your source; it comes from the source of all power, the one Being. In the vast ocean of infinite consciousness there is infinite power, and it is yours on demand. Most of it you may never need to use, but it is yours all the same.

If you can hold on to the essence of Being at the root of your being, if you can anchor yourself in its infinite wisdom, you will have real power. When you are firmly established in the knowledge of your true self, the nature and purpose of existence is understood, and immense power is generated. This kind of power leads to greatness, success, and a life free of suffering.

Take a moment to become aware of who is reading this book. Do you feel a presence? That presence is not your mind; it's your soul. The mind might be saying, *What am I going to have for lunch?* or *I wonder what time it is.* The inner dialogue happens in the presence of the soul. Thoughts come and go, feelings come and go. The molecules of the body come and go. But they come and go in this presence.

This presence, the soul, recycles itself as your memories, your moods, and even your personality, because you don't have the same personality today that you had when you were five years of age, or when you were fifteen. It would indeed be a sorry state if you did. Your personality is an expression of the evolving universe; it's constantly changing, growing, evolving, transforming. Everything in your life is constantly transforming, but it's transforming in a presence that's always there. That presence was there when you were a newborn baby, it was there when you were a little girl or a little boy, it was there when you were an adolescent, just as it's there right now. And it will be there tomorrow when you are very old.

Who is going through this experience? The real you — the you that we call *pure consciousness, the field of intelligence, the inner self, the soul, the spirit, the infinite consciousness, the Being within you*. Here, we have used all of these terms synonymously. If you get in touch with this presence, if you really become intimate with it because it's your own inner self, then you will know experientially, without anybody telling you, that this presence was there before you were born, and it will be there after you die.

There is an ancient saying from India about the soul: "Fire cannot burn it, water cannot wet it, wind cannot dry it, weapons cannot cleave it. It's ancient, it's unborn, and it never dies." The soul is the source of all reality, but the domain of the soul is beyond your everyday reality. That's why you need to experience the domain of your soul to stay in touch with your soul, to experience the qualities of the *real* you.

How do you experience the domain of your soul? By spending time in silence, by quieting the time-bound conversation in your head and tuning in to the timeless, peaceful quiet of your soul. When you experience complete silence in your body-mind, then you recognize that you are not your thoughts but the Being who is having the thoughts.

Slowly, by spending time in silence, you notice that the scenery comes and goes, but the seer is always there. You realize that you are not the scenery; you are the seer, the witness of the scenery. As you shift your identity from the scenery to the seer, everything starts to slowly awaken. You glimpse the soul, and you begin to experience more expansive states of consciousness: cosmic consciousness, divine consciousness, unity consciousness.

By spending time in silence, you begin to realize that no matter what the scenery is, you are painting it. You have always painted it. In the past you did it unconsciously, randomly, chaotically. Now, like a great Michelangelo or Leonardo da Vinci, you consciously create a masterpiece that influences your destiny and the destiny of others.

As we have seen, when you want something to become your life experience, you put your attention on it. So if you want to experience the reality of your soul, then put your attention on your soul. Take your attention off the world of the intellect and the ego, and tune in to your soul. Commune with your soul. Feel your soul. Just being in the silence of your soul will connect you with your source. And how do you know that you are connected to your source? Certain signs tell you that you are connected, that you are living from the source. And you can monitor your spiritual progress by paying attention to these signs.

The first sign that you are living from the source is a lack of worry. You don't worry about anything.

If you're connected to the source, what is there to worry about? So you feel lighthearted, happy. You don't get offended by the comments of others, you don't feel obsessive about having your own way, and you don't experience resistance to what is. You experience effortless ease, spontaneity, and no resistance to whatever is happening around you.

The second sign that you are living from the source is the experience of synchronicity and meaningful coincidence. Why synchronicity and coincidence? Because both of these are expressions of the infinite organizing power of pure consciousness. Synchronicity and coincidence are orchestrated in the place beyond space, time, and causality — the domain of the soul known as *infinite correlation,* where things happen at the same time. *Chronos* means time, and when everything is *synchronized in time,* or coincidental, then you know it's a message from your soul.

Coincidence means many incidents happening together that would not likely happen together; it is a conspiracy of improbable events. Though a coincidence may seem to be an accident, in truth there is no such thing as an accident or random event. What we call *an accident,* or *a random event,* is the nonlocal correlation of the universal mind. Every event is being orchestrated by infinite consciousness, and every event is a conspiracy of an infinity of events. For anything to happen in your body, in your mind, in your life, the entire universe has to conspire.

Though we may not understand it, the essential truth of the universe is that it's synchronistic and coincidental. Everything is connected with everything else, and if we are in synch with the universe, then we experience synchronicity. The more connected we are, the more we experience coincident or simultaneous events.

Therefore, never ignore coincidences. When a coincidence happens, ask yourself, *What does this mean? What is the significance of this coincidence?* Coincidences are messages from your soul; they are clues to the nonlocal Self. The local self is the person that you think you are. The nonlocal Self is the unbounded spirit. You experience both, so when coincidence happens, in that moment you have glimpsed your soul, the nonlocal Self. When you have a conscious awareness of your soul, you experience everything as a miracle. You feel happy, and your life begins to transform. You see the connection between your inner world and your outer world; you see that every event in your life is being orchestrated by the entire universe.

And when you realize this fact, your mind reels with bewilderment and astonishment at the miracle of spirit. This bewilderment produces gratitude, and gratitude activates even more miracles. This shifts you into a higher state of consciousness. As you elevate your attention from the world of the humdrum and trivial to the world of the magical and miraculous, your life becomes magical and miraculous. Your attention is spontaneously alert to the fact that life itself is a miracle. And the more you put your attention on miracles, the more you become the conscious creator of miracles.

Lastly, the third sign that you are living from the source is that you know yourself as a creator, not a victim. You realize that the world is a mirror of your thoughts, your feelings, your desires, your interpretations. You know that every situation, every relationship, every event you experience is mirroring something inside you. When you don't like what's happening in your world, you don't try to correct it by looking outside yourself. That would be like polishing the leaves of a plant instead of watering the roots.

If something you're experiencing in life is causing you to be unhappy, you recognize that it's your creation. Otherwise, you stay in the victim mode: *Poor me. This is happening to me, and I am powerless to change it.* Why wait for the world to change when, in fact, you are creating the world? Whatever is happening is because you are creating it, so you ask yourself, *What do I need to shift inside of me so this doesn't happen?*

No problem on Earth can be solved by addressing it at the level of the problem, but every problem can be solved at the level of spirit. So you go beyond the world of illusion, the mask of appearances, to the invisible world of spirit. In the world of spirit, you find the creator of both the personal body-mind and the cosmic body-mind. At this level, you do not even struggle with the problem; you rise above the problem. And in doing so, you create a new solution.

No circumstance can overshadow the experience of unboundedness that comes from experiencing pure consciousness. And the only way to really experience pure consciousness is to transcend thought and enter into silent communion with your soul.

∽

The Experience and Practice of Power

Spend Time in Silent Communion with Your Soul

If you were to ask me what I consider the most important experience of my life, I would say it is the experience of transcending to a place of stillness and silence — twice a day, every day. Through meditation, I experience the state of Being that is the ground state of my body-mind, of my life. So to me, this is one of the most important things we can do to evolve to a higher state of consciousness.

Take a minute right now to close your eyes. When you close your eyes, thoughts automatically start to come, right? If I ask you to do nothing except sit and close your eyes, one of your biggest complaints is likely to be "I have too many thoughts." This is great, because most people won't have this complaint. They just act out their thoughts, and they aren't even aware that they are not their thoughts. So the first thing you learn through silent meditation is that the "I am" is witnessing your thoughts.

Then, as you witness the effortless way that thoughts start to come, you introduce a mantra. What is a mantra? A mantra is a sound or nonverbal incantation that you mentally repeat over and over again without moving your tongue or your lips. General mantras include "so-hum," "ah-hum," or just "I am." By repeating the mantra, what happens is that your thoughts interfere with the mantra, and the mantra interferes with your thoughts. Then, if you just stay in that feeling, in that state of stillness, sometimes the thoughts and the mantra totally cancel each other out. This is when you slip into the silent gap between thoughts.

In the gap between thoughts, you become the witness, the observer. From here you can observe your thoughts, feelings, emotions, and reactions. As the witness, you observe without labels, definitions, descriptions, analysis, evaluation, or judgment. Krishnamurti, the great Indian philosopher, said that the highest form of human intelligence is the ability to observe yourself and not judge yourself.

Keep observing, keep observing, until you enter the soul's domain. Here you witness the presence of spirit in everything you see, hear, smell, taste, and touch. At this level, there is only one witness, one Being, and the whole universe is the physical body of that Being. In the soul's domain, you have a heightened sense of knowingness, and you can eavesdrop on the cosmic mind. This is when questions answer themselves, and problems solve themselves because the ego's world is transformed into the world of spirit, pure potentiality, and infinite possibilities.

By spending time in silent communion with your soul, you gain knowledge of the Self, the maker of reality. This kind of knowledge cannot come to you through books or in universities of learning; this is a knowledge that you become. When you become this knowledge, you are free of grasping, clinging, repulsion, fear, and flight. You are free of both past and future. In this knowledge, you are empowered, you are free, and you live in grace.

I encourage you to make a commitment to enjoy periods of silence and solitude, to be with yourself, to connect with and enjoy nature, to be happy in quiet surroundings. Make a practice of sitting in silence or meditation every day. Sitting in silent meditation quiets the mind, and allows you to go past the dark alleys and ghost-filled attics of the mind, into the world of the transcendent. By spending time in silent meditation, you cultivate the peace of inner silence.

Studies have shown that when people meditate their physical and emotional health is measurably improved, including lower blood pressure, greater resistance to disease, less stressful response to challenging situations, better work performance, greater self esteem, and more nourishing relationships. People who have practiced regular meditation for five years have a biological age that is twelve years younger than their chronological age. But the most important reason to meditate is to connect with your soul.

The soul is the domain of your awareness where you are simultaneously personal and universal. When you connect with your soul, you connect with the field of intelligence that is orchestrating the infinite and diverse activity of the universe. The more you connect with your soul, the more you become the alert witness of your thoughts and feelings, your aspirations, your intentions and desires, and even the nuances of change that appear as comfort and discomfort in your body.

In the seamless web of intelligence where everything is connected with everything else, even the slightest disturbance in one part of the field affects the whole web of life. If you are sensitive and alert to the fluctuations in the microcosm that is you, then you are more alert to how these fluctuations affect the macrocosm that is the universe. As a result of this awareness, you consciously choose to align yourself with the most evolutionary impulses of intelligence that are manifesting as the infinite diversity of the universe.

Uni-verse, being a melody or a song as the word implies, is one verse, one song. *Di-verse* means many songs or different verses of the same melody. When you align yourself with the infinite *diversity* of the *universe*, your personal desires harmonize with the desires of the one mind. They become more evolutionary because the one mind moves in the direction of increasing evolution. An evolutionary desire is one that brings simultaneous fulfillment to all those who are affected by the desire. So even though your individual desire is going to benefit you personally, it's also going to ripple across the ocean of universal consciousness and simultaneously benefit all those who are affected by it.

One technique for entering the soul's domain is to close your eyes and go into silence, or meditation, for twenty minutes. After twenty minutes of silence, open your eyes and invite your favorite archetypes, your heroes and heroines, to come and express themselves through you. You might relate to a religious figure, such as Buddha, Jesus Christ, Mother Mary, or Mohammed. You might relate to your spiritual ancestors or to one of the mythological gods and goddesses of antiquity. Begin by asking yourself, *Who are my role models, my heroes or heroines in history, in mythology, in religion? Who inspires me? They are the seeds of greatness in me.*

During the rest of the day, feel the sensations in your body, and whenever you feel challenged or in trouble, ask your role models to incarnate through you and to guide you. Then, before you go to sleep at night, witness the whole day and tell yourself, *It's already a dream. It's gone.* Just observe what happened throughout the day. Don't analyze it, don't evaluate it, don't judge it. Just witness the day and say, *It's gone.* Then say to yourself, *Just as I witnessed the day, I'm going to witness my dreams.* When you wake up in the morning and remember your dreams, just say, *It's gone.*

Spending time in silence and solitude allows you to escape the prison of the intellect, and awaken from the hypnosis of social conditioning. As you quiet the mind, you enter the realm of pure consciousness. The realm of pure consciousness is infinitely silent and infinitely dynamic at the same time; it is pure creativity in its essence. In silence and solitude, you are being with the one Being, and this puts you into harmony with the cosmos.

In silence and solitude, you never feel lonely, because loneliness is an alienation from everything. In silence and solitude, you experience a connectedness with everything. And this connectedness, this living from the source, is the key to power.

Pay Attention to the Qualities of Pure Consciousness

Another thing I would suggest is to look at the qualities of pure consciousness, and on a given day hold one of them in your awareness. What are the qualities of pure consciousness? They are the qualities that structure the infinite diversity of the universe. In your simplest state of awareness, they are your qualities as well. Some of the qualities of pure consciousness are pure potentiality, infinite possibilities, infinite silence, pure knowledge, freedom, flexibility, unboundedness, self-sufficiency, self-referring, fully awake within itself, infinite dynamism, infinite creativity, infinite correlation, infinite organizing power, perfect balance, evolutionary, nourishing, harmonizing, simple, blissful, and invincible.

On one given day, for example, you could hold the quality of freedom in your awareness. What does it mean to hold freedom in your awareness? It means you don't try to analyze or interpret the notion of freedom. You just put your attention on the quality of freedom, that's all. Just keep freedom alive in your awareness, and watch how things change in your life. Be a silent witness to freedom, and that alone will spontaneously give you insight into the mechanics of freedom. Slowly, over a period of time, this practice will spontaneously give you the experience of freedom.

Then, on another day, select another quality and hold it in your awareness. As you put your attention on the qualities of pure consciousness, they will spontaneously cause changes in your physiology and manifest as your reality.

Never Stop Asking Questions

If you want a simple prescription for accessing the field of intelligence, then every morning before you enter into a period of silence or meditation, put your attention on your heart and ask yourself, *Who am I? What do I want?* Ask yourself these questions, and then listen. The universe is a field of possibilities that is compelled to make choices when you ask questions of it. There's no need to go looking for the answers. The moment you ask these questions, the answers start to appear. In asking these two questions, you invite the field of infinite possibilities to make the choices for you. Just ask, and something will happen. Some clue will start to appear in your life that answers these questions. The answers may come to you in the form of an insight, an inspiration, a chance encounter, a sudden creative impulse. The answers may come through synchronicity and coincidence, a relationship, a situation, a circumstance, or an event.

Some other questions you can ask yourself are: What is my purpose in life? What contribution can I make to my family, to my society, to my world? What are my unique talents, and how can I express them in the service of humanity? What brings me peak experiences and joy? What are the qualities that I look for in a friend? What qualities do I want to express in my relationships?

Keep asking questions, and then allow the answers to incubate. This period of incubation allows the cosmic computer, the essence of infinite consciousness and infinite correlation, to compute the infinity of details in the complexity of the situation and give you the right answer.

By asking questions, you begin to explore the many domains of your existence. And to whom do you address these questions? Your own inner self. The poet Rumi says, "The whole universe exists inside you; ask all from yourself." All fulfillment comes from the creativity of your soul; there is nothing that cannot be solved by allowing your soul to find a creative solution to it.

Never stop asking questions. Don't look for answers but ask questions. Ask, and you shall receive. The power asleep in all of us doesn't awaken until we call it.

Key Points

To experience and practice power:

- Spend time in silent communion with your soul.
- Pay attention to the qualities of pure consciousness.
- Never stop asking questions.

· 10 ·

What is freedom and how do I experience it?

*Free · dom (frē' dəm): The power to think or act
without restraint; the capacity to exercise choice.*

One of the most crucial aspects of life is the
notion of freedom and the notion of bondage.
Ultimately, our goal is to experience freedom, but to
understand what freedom is we first have to understand what bondage is. What does it mean to be free
and what does it mean to be in bondage?

To be in bondage is to be stuck in this or that
possibility, having lost the ability to choose from an

infinite range of responses. What is the bondage to? The bondage is always to our own boundaries, to our own beliefs and conditioned responses. Boundaries and beliefs are nothing more than ideas or concepts that we have committed to and accepted as truth. And when they are as rigid and inflexible as concrete, we cannot see past them. They become the prison walls that we inadvertently construct around ourselves.

You wrap yourself in thoughts the way a spider wraps flies in gossamer. You are both the spider and the fly, entangling yourself in your own web. Your entire lifetime and other lifetimes are packaged inside you as imprints or energy patterns that are triggered by words, encounters, and relationships. You have been conditioned to interpret your experiences in a certain way, and this determines how you react to them. So any bondage that you experience is really the prison of your own conditioning.

Most people live their entire lives in bondage. They are a bundle of nerves and conditioned responses, which are constantly being triggered by other people and circumstances into totally predictable outcomes. To be free of bondage, we have to break down conditioned responses; we have to go beyond boundaries and experience the boundless.

What is freedom? Freedom comes from the experiential knowledge of our true nature, which is already free. It comes from finding out that our real essence is the joyful field of infinite consciousness that animates all of creation. To have the experience of that silent witness is just to be. Then we are free. In this state of freedom, we understand that life is the meaningful coexistence of all opposite values. We may experience happiness or we may experience pain and suffering, but we do not get attached to pleasure and we do not recoil in fear of pain. In freedom, we even lose our fear of death, because the belief in mortality is just a spell that we have cast upon ourselves.

Behind the mask of mortality is the field of immortality. The real you is immortal; it is beyond birth and death. The real you is not your ego, which is time-bound; it is your spirit, which is timeless.

When you know that, when you identify with your spirit, you are free of every limitation, including the limitation that you are a person trapped inside a body for the span of a lifetime. You are the source of both body and mind, and you are not touched by this world of change because you know that you are the unchanging essence of pure consciousness itself.

The time-bound comes and goes; the timeless always is. The time-bound is the known; the timeless is the fresh unknown. In our addiction to the time-bound, we have projected a reality of separation and suffering. We live in a collective nightmare, a collective hallucination where we are bound and imprisoned by our own projections. Past and future are in the imagination; reality is in this moment. Suffering is in the imagination; freedom is in this moment. Beyond all of the obstacles to freedom is a world that is free of all projection; it is the world of infinite consciousness. And that world abides in the eternal moment.

There never was a time when your life was not this moment. There never will be a time when your life is not this moment. It is impossible to deal with that which does not exist in this moment. Therefore, live in this moment by keeping your attention in this moment. Abide in this moment, and you will abide in that which is eternal, timeless, ageless, and fresh.

The universe is experiencing itself from an infinity of perspectives, this moment. One of these perspectives is you, in this moment. You are infinite, unbounded — nowhere in particular but everywhere at the same time. Nowhere is also *now here*. When you live in the *now* and the *here,* you recognize that the real you dwells in the timeless, eternal moment. You no longer want to live in the memories of the past or the imaginings of the future. You want to live in the present moment, where you can exercise the power and freedom of choice.

The whole purpose of living in freedom is to enjoy the choices that you make in every successive moment of the present. People have asked me, "Is the world one of free will, or is it deterministic?" The world is both deterministic and one of free will.

If you are aware and beyond conditioning, then you have free will and you live in freedom. But if you are unaware and conditioned, then you do not have free will and your world is deterministic.

The present is the moment of choice and interpretation. Your choices, this moment, are creating the external events you are experiencing in this moment. Your interpretations, this moment, are creating the internal events you are experiencing in this moment. And because the "outer" world is a mirror of your "inner" world, your choices and interpretations co-create and perpetuate one another. Remember, you are neither the choice nor the interpretation but the source of both. The key ingredient is, therefore, silent witnessing. Become aware of your choices and interpretations, and you will begin to experience freedom of choice.

The silent witness is awareness itself. Awareness, aware of itself, is presence, profound wisdom, and peace. Therefore, the key to freedom is to live in self-referred consciousness, which means to identify with your inner self instead of your self-image. Within this freedom lies the ability to spontaneously put your attention on those choices that bring joy to you, and also joy to others.

THE EXPERIENCE AND PRACTICE OF FREEDOM

Practice Life-Centered, Present-Moment Awareness

Come out of the prison of time-bound awareness and enter the world of the timeless and free. The prison of time-bound awareness is the world of separation and suffering. The world of the timeless is the world of pure consciousness, where every moment is free. This moment is free because all your troubles live in the past or in the future, which means they live in your imagination.

When a situation is troubling you, then ask yourself, *What's wrong right now?* If you do this, then you realize that in this moment there are no problems. Separate the situation from the moment, because the situation will pass, while the moment will remain. The situation always transforms, but every moment remains perfect and unchanged.

Keep your attention on this moment. This moment is the *only* moment you have the power to act. You cannot take action in the past or in the future, so if you dwell on the past or on the future, you feel powerless. Life is in this moment. Therefore, live in this moment. Act in this moment. Intend in this moment. Detach from worry in this moment. Stay in this moment. This is life-centered, present-moment awareness.

You can make this moment an act of beauty and perfection by practicing life-centered, present-moment awareness. Now is the door to eternity, and when you live in the moment, you live from the source. In every moment, the door is open to the source. The source has never left you, but you can overlook it with your memories of the past and your imaginings of the future. If your attention is in the moment, if you pay attention to what is, then you see the fullness in every moment. This is within your power right now, because the only time you have is now.

Now is the moment that never ends. When the past happened, it happened now. When the future happens, it happens now. The present is the only moment that never ends, because the present is timeless and immeasurable. The present is infinite consciousness being all that was, all that is, and all that will be.

What is, is the activity of the total universe, this moment. For anything to happen, the whole universe has to be happening the way it's happening. Every event in life is a conspiracy of the entire universe, so if you resist this moment, you resist the entire universe. Remember that difficult situations don't create suffering; resistance to what is creates suffering. When you experience resistance, your unconscious mind is perceiving a situation as intolerable. Your resistance, however, only perpetuates the situation because your attention is on the problem.

Even if a situation is unpleasant, separate the situation from this moment, and surrender to the moment.

To surrender is to join the flow of life. The situation that surrounds this moment may be intolerable, but this moment is still perfect. By surrendering to this moment and doing whatever the situation demands, you are established in Being while performing action. This is to be in the world and not of it.

When you surrender to this moment, you act from the level of your soul. And when you act from the level of your soul, you take the appropriate action in this moment. You act without being compulsively driven by a memory of resentment or being wronged. When you act from the level of your soul, you act like a true spiritual warrior — without anger, self-righteousness, resentment, or grievances.

Learn to act moment by moment as the detached silent witness, and you will act with spontaneous right action, and with timing and finesse. This action is free from bondage, and it doesn't entail suffering. The situation will change, moment by moment; that is the will of the one Being. But if you flow with the moment, your will becomes aligned with the will of the one Being. If you surrender to the moment, you act without expectations, but certainly with an intended outcome. An intended outcome without expectations or attachment orchestrates its own fulfillment. This is because the power of the whole universe is behind the intention, this moment. The universe only operates in the eternal now. So when you execute this moment with full awareness, then you move with the evolutionary impulse of the universe. You do what needs to be done in this moment with impeccability, and leave the results to the unknown.

Whenever you feel resistance, just observe the resistance; then surrender to what is. If you find yourself unable to surrender to a difficult situation, then surrender to your pain and suffering. Witness your pain and suffering. Do not think about the pain; feel the pain. The source is wholeness. It wants to heal you and lift your pain, not by abolishing painful memories but by putting you totally in the present, where the past does not exist. If you can be totally life-centered in this moment, then you are free.

One technique that will help you to live in each moment with awareness, with lightness, with ease, is observing your breath. Your breath is neither in the past nor in the future; it is only in this moment. With every breath that you breathe in, the infinite consciousness comes to you. With every breath that you breathe out, you go to the infinite consciousness. And in the space between the in-breath and the out-breath, you abide in the infinite consciousness. In reality, there is no going nor coming; you are eternally in the flow.

Just witness your breath, and practice life-centered, present-moment awareness. If you can do this, you move into a domain of consciousness where you have your attention on what is, where you feel the presence of spirit and see the fullness of every moment.

The entire universe is spinning out of nothingness, now. Behind all the noise and activity of your life is silence and stillness, now. The power of pure consciousness is present, now. The freedom of the boundless, timeless spirit is present, now. The grace of the simple, unaffected beauty of life is present, now.

The poet Rumi says, "Past and future veil God from our sight; burn up both of them with the fire of presence." God's presence is in this moment, and time is the only obstacle to God.

Observe Your Addictive Behaviors Without Judgment

Most human behavior is nothing other than the avoidance of pain and the pursuit of pleasure. Whenever we experience an event, whether it's a visit to the dentist or going on a joyride at the carnival, our consciousness registers that experience internally on a spectrum with great pain at one end and extreme pleasure at the other. Once completed, the memory of that experience is tagged to either pain or pleasure, and it continues to exist in our body-mind.

Memory is useful because it gives us a sense of continuity. But memory is also imprisoning because it conditions us in predictable ways. The great yogi Lord Shiva said, "I use memories, but I do not allow memories to use me." We have to use memories;

otherwise we wouldn't find our way home. When we use memories, we are creators. But when our memories use us, we become victims.

Your spirit is inviting you to step out of the prison of memory and conditioned responses into the experience of freedom. And the next step in the flight to freedom is to observe your addictive behaviors without judgment. Addiction is the number-one disease of civilization, and it's directly and indirectly related to all other diseases. Besides physical addictions, such as the addiction to food, tobacco, alcohol, and drugs, there are psychological addictions, such as the addiction to work, to sex, to television, to shopping, to appearing young, to control, to suffering, to anxiety, to melodrama, to perfection.

Why are we addicted to all these things? We are addicted because we are not living from our source; we have lost our connection to our soul. The use of food, alcohol, or drugs is essentially a material response to a need that is not really physical at its foundation. Drunkenness, for example, is really a forgetting of personal memory so we can experience the joy of the nonpersonal, the universal. What we are looking for is pure joy rather than mere sensation, or even oblivion of sensation. Self-destructive behavior is unrecognized spiritual craving. All addictions are really a search for the exultation of spirit, and this search has to do with the expansion of consciousness, the intoxication of love, which is pure consciousness.

Over and over, people have tried to overcome their addictions through psychological and behavioral methods or through medication. None of these offers a permanent cure. The only cure for addiction is spiritual. We hunger for the ecstatic experience, which is a need as basic as the need for food, water, or shelter. *Ecstasy*, or *ekstasis*, literally means stepping out. True ecstasy is stepping out of the bondage of the time-bound, space-bound world of materialism. We long to step out of the limitations of the body. We long to be free of fear and limitation. We hunger for the oblivion of our ego so that we can experience our infinite Being.

Start today to transcend your addictive behaviors by observing them without judgment. Wake every day with a prayer: "Thank you, God, for making me just as I am," and then observe yourself. Be a witness to your thoughts, your moods, your reactions, your behaviors. They represent your memories of the past, and by witnessing them in the present, you liberate yourself of the past. By observing your addictive behaviors, you observe your conditioning. And when you observe your conditioning, you are free of it, because you are not your conditioning; you are the observer of your conditioning.

Observe the silence between your thoughts, your actions, your reactions, and you will feel the presence of spirit in the stillness of those spaces. In the mere observation of yourself, you begin the process of healing and transformation. And if you keep practicing ever-present awareness of your own self, then insight, intuition, imagination, and intention begin to blossom.

People have asked me, "If the universe is so elegantly organized and we are born with all this human potential and creativity, then why are we so ignorant?"

Well, if we were already enlightened, there would be nothing to do. It's a process. If you occasionally succumb to your addictive behavior, understand that this, too, is part of the process. You may keep falling, but you can always get up and continue on your journey.

No matter how hysterical your environment appears to be, remain alert and sober in your ever-present witnessing awareness. Resolve not to get drawn into the melodrama around you. Remind yourself, *I am neither superior nor inferior to anyone who exists. Saint or sinner, the spirit that resides within me is the divine spirit. It has taken on a certain role in this lifetime; it has taken on other roles in other lifetimes. I honor the divine spirit in myself and in all beings as holy and sacred no matter what role it is playing.*

None of us are the roles we play. Recognizing this truth, it is easier to forgive all perceived transgressions. We don't feel compelled to label, evaluate, analyze, or judge ourselves or others. When we have no need to label or judge, it's easier to relinquish the desire to control and manipulate others.

By knowing the true nature of reality, it is possible to go beyond suffering. When you go beyond suffering, you help others to go beyond suffering. As you continue on your journey of healing, you help others to heal. And you can start to heal by observing your addictive behaviors without judgment. Once you find your true self, once you become whole, the only intoxication you have is the intoxication of pure consciousness, pure Being.

Transcend Your Fear of the Unknown

Within every moment, there lies a junction point between the unknown and the known. In that junction point the unknown transforms into the known. What is the known? The known is everything that has already happened. As soon as you say "known," it's in the past; it's gone. The known is a memory. And what is the unknown? The unknown is the field of all possibilities in every successive moment of the present. The unknown is the unlimited and the free.

You are in the unknown at this moment, and everything from this moment onward is the unknown. In fact, you live and breathe and function in the unknown all the time, while pretending that it's the known. And by attaching yourself to a pretense, to an illusion, you lose touch with what is real and begin to fear the transient and unreal, including death.

Most people fear the unknown, when they should really be afraid of the known. To live in the known is to live in the prison of the past, and therefore in the imagination. The known is an illusion. The real reality is the unknown, so why not live in what is actually real? When we step into the unknown, we are free of the past. When we step into the unknown, we are free of every limitation because fresh choices are available in every moment of our existence.

Pure consciousness is infinitely flexible and unbounded; this is the nature of Being. Conditioned thinking is inflexible; it is bound by our attachment to ideas, notions, beliefs. Freedom is the experience of the unbounded. When you are truly free, you are infinitely flexible in any situation. This flexibility gives you an inner stability that no other experience can overshadow.

Freedom implies acceptance, letting come what comes and letting go what goes. Freedom implies letting go of the known and having the willingness and confidence to step into the great unknown in every moment of your life. Even when it comes to death, do not think about death, do not fear death, but die to every moment. When St. Paul said, "Die unto death," he meant die to the past in every moment. Step into what is happening right now, and you die to both the past and the future. If you can do this right now, you can even conquer the fear of death.

Don't let imagined fears of the future influence the present. And don't let memories of the past influence the present. Be fresh. Every child who is born is the universe looking at itself with fresh eyes. When you look at the universe with fresh eyes, you are dying to the known. If you can step out of the river of memory and conditioning and see the world as if for the first time in this moment, then you can create a new world in this moment.

This moment is a moment of power where the universe re-creates itself. To dive into this moment is to dive into the unknown becoming the known. The unknown is the fresh feel of infinite possibilities. It is Being becoming, transforming, evolving. Every moment that you live is a moment that is overflowing with possibilities.

Once you have broken the shackles of your own bondage, you can impart your own reality to every event in your life. In this state of freedom, you are no longer mired in the tyranny of an imagined past or the fear of an anticipated future. In this state of freedom, you experience truth, beauty, goodness, harmony.

The poet Rumi says, "We are tasting the taste, this moment, of eternity." Transcend your fear of the unknown by keeping your attention on the present moment. Taste this moment as a moment of eternity, and you will taste the experience of freedom.

KEY POINTS

To experience and practice freedom:

- Practice life-centered, present-moment awareness.
- Observe your addictive behaviors without judgment.
- Transcend your fear of the unknown.

· II ·

What is grace and how do I live it?

Grace (grās): The effortless flow of existence;
love and favor freely bestowed on us.

Grace is the effortless flow of existence that comes when you are living in harmony with life, when the rhythms of your body-mind are in synch with nature's rhythms. To live in grace is to experience that state of consciousness where things flow and your desires are easily fulfilled. Grace is magical, synchronistic, coincidental, joyful. It's that good-luck factor.

And how do you live in grace? It's simple. Just allow the universe to flow through you without interfering.

In the speck of DNA that created your body is the intelligence that informs you that you are an ancient being. This intelligence has infinite organizing power because it's the same intelligence that orchestrates the movement of the cosmos. One hundred trillion cells instantly communicate with one another in every moment. These one hundred trillion cells came out of one living cell born of information from two cells, and they only had to multiply fifty times to create all the cells of your body.

You are a miracle of evolution, a biological organism delicate and fragile and yet tenacious because you have survived throughout eons of cosmic cycles. You are what you are because the universe is what it is. The universe is what it is because you are what you are. The body you inhabit may seem to be your personal possession, but in truth it belongs to the universe.

Your DNA encodes the experiences of your ancestors, both human and animal. It contains the knowledge that taught you as an amphibian how to fly and become a bird, and as a primate how to create language and art and science so you could be human. Your body recycles itself, bringing some of the old with every birth so that the knowledge encoded in the wisdom of the universe is never lost. At the same time, it brings a fresh perspective so you can build on the old and give yourself the opportunity for creativity.

Moment by moment your body sculpts a neural landscape that records every experience of your life. In this very moment, the creative potential that you actualize in your neural networks is converting memory and purpose into biological response. In every breath you take, the universe is born anew. It looks at itself with new eyes, new perspective, and a freshly born sense of wonder.

Knowing all this, treat your body with reverence and take care of it. Nurture your body with your loving attention. Nourish your body with healthy food and fresh water. Feed your body with the freshness of the earth, and the colors of the rainbow that the earth offers in the form of fruits and vegetables. Drink deeply of the Earth's waters so that you open the lines of communication and intelligence that course through your tissues and blood vessels. Breathe deeply so that your lungs are fully expanded with air.

Make a commitment to keep your body free of toxins, both physical and emotional. Don't contaminate your body with dead food and drink, toxic chemicals, toxic relationships, or toxic emotions in the form of anger, fear, or guilt. Make sure that you nurture healthy relationships, and that you do not harbor resentments or grievances. The health of every cell directly contributes to your state of well-being, because every cell is a point of awareness within the field of awareness that is you.

Let your body dance with the universe. Let go of all constriction and tightness in your consciousness so that your body can relax into the rhythms of the universe. Move your body, exercise your body, and keep it moving. The more you dance with the universe, the more joy, vitality, energy, creativity, synchronicity, and harmony you will experience. And when your body asks for rest and renewal, listen to its voice.

Rabindranath Tagore summarizes the miracle of life more beautifully than science can explain it. He says, "The same stream of life that runs through my veins night and day runs through the world and dances in rhythmic measures. It is the same life that shoots in joy through the dust of the earth in number- less blades of grass, and breaks into tumultuous waves of leaves and flowers. It is the same life that is rocked in the ocean-cradle of birth and of death, in ebb and in flow. I feel my limbs are made glorious by the touch of this world of life. And my pride is from the life-throb of ages dancing in my blood this moment."

The oceans and rivers of this biosphere are the lifeblood that circulates in your heart and in your body. The air is the sacred breath of life that gives energy to every cell in your body, so that it may live and breathe and participate in the dance of the cos-mos. To have the experience of "the life-throb of ages dancing in your blood this moment" is to have the experience of joy, the experience of connectedness to the cosmos. This is the healing experience; it is the experience of being whole. And to be whole is to live in grace.

∽

The Experience and Practice of Grace

Listen to Your Body's Wisdom

Can you experience this moment as the life-throb of ages dancing in every cell of your body? Can you realize with deep conviction that you are the earth, water, fire, air, and void of space? Can you feel this and know this in the depths of your being? If so, then listen to your body's wisdom.

Your body is constantly speaking to you through signals of comfort and discomfort, pleasure and pain, attraction and repulsion. When you listen to the subtle nuances of sensation in your body, you are accessing intuitive intelligence. This intelligence is contextual, relational, nurturing, holistic, and wise.

Intuitive intelligence is more accurate and precise than anything that exists in the realm of rational thought. Intuition is not a thought; it is the nonlocal cosmic field of information that whispers to you in the silence between your thoughts. So when you listen to the inner intelligence of your body, which is the ultimate and supreme genius, you are eavesdropping on the universe and accessing information that most people don't normally access.

Science has shown that the cells of the body are holograms of the universe, which means that all the information that can possibly be known in the universe is encoded in the cellular structure of each cell. Every part of a hologram contains all the information of the whole — that's why it's called a *hologram*. Intuition is nothing but a heightened sense of awareness that comes from familiarity with the information fields in your own body. This information is encoded holographically in every cell of your body. And if you just access a little more information, you become, by common standards, intuitive.

Listen to your body's wisdom. Become aware of the sensations in your body, and you will know the whole cosmos, because the whole cosmos is experienced as sensations in your body. In reality, these sensations are the voice of spirit, which speaks to you at the finest level of feeling in your body. When you offer your body your deep listening, you will hear the voice of spirit, because your body is a biocomputer that is constantly plugged into the cosmic psyche. Your body has a computing ability that can instantly take into account the infinity of details that create every event in your life. It has a win-win orientation, and it solves all problems at a more expansive level of awareness than the one in which the problems arose.

The next time you need to make a decision, rather than trying to understand it intellectually, pay attention to the sensations of comfort or discomfort in your body, and go with your intuitive feelings. Intellectual understanding is all right, but it's not always the ultimate test of whether you're making the right decision. Before making a choice, ask your body, *How do you feel about this?* If your body sends a signal of comfort and eagerness, proceed. If your body sends a signal of physical or emotional distress, watch out. When confronted with any situation, ask your body whether it feels comfortable or not. If the sensation in your body feels good when you do something, then that's the right decision. If there's an uncomfortable sensation in your body, then it's not the right thing to do.

When you are out of harmony with universal rhythms, the signal that will come to you is a sense of discomfort, whether it's physical, mental, or emotional. When you are flowing in harmony with the universe, the signal that will come to you is a sense of comfort, ease, or joy. When you're relaxed and you're going with the flow of the universe, then from heartbeat to heartbeat there is something called *variability*, which is a natural variation that goes with the flexible nature of the universe. It's easy, it's flowing, and the autonomic nervous system dominates. But when you're stressed, when you have too much adrenaline, the heart beats like soldiers marching in step.

The heart is not just a pump; it's an organ that feels and thinks. But unlike the rational mind, it feels and thinks intuitively and creatively with love, compassion, interconnectedness, and inseparability. Your heart beats because of something called a *pacemaker*. The pacemaker is not a single cell; it is one hundred cells firing at the same time, with the same frequency, to the same tune. Every cell has an electrical impulse, and one hundred cells have to fire coherently to create the pacemaker.

The more flexibility and variability in your heart from beat to beat, the more you create a coherent electromagnetic field. When this happens, then the rest of the cells fall into that coherence, and you radiate a coherent field of electromagnetic energy, which is the *aura*. The aura is just the coherence or radiance of your heart. You radiate that energy field to the universe, and when that energy field is coherent, you align with the elements and forces of the universe. Once you join that flow, your every intention becomes aligned or in synch with the activity of the universe. This is very powerful because the activity of the universe is your own inner self that is coming from a much deeper level of existence. So if you have a "heart's desire," allow your intention to come from the depths of your being, where your soul is localizing as your heart. Put your attention on your heart, even momentarily, and if you feel love, compassion, peace, harmony, or laughter, this will create a coherent electromagnetic field. Then just let your impulses emerge from your heart, from the depths of your being, and the desire will orchestrate its own fulfillment.

Maintain Inner-Body Awareness at All Times

The only way to know a person or anything else in the so-called external world is through feeling your body. Therefore, develop a sensual relationship with your body by maintaining inner-body awareness at all times. In any interaction with another person, pay attention to your body. When looking at others, feel your body. When listening to others, feel your body; listen with your *whole* body. Feel your whole body as a single energy field of intelligence: alive, vibrant, joyful.

Inhabit your body fully by bringing your awareness into your body. Be alive in your body. Feel the presence of spirit in your body. Commune with the presence of spirit in your body. When you are centered in your body, when your spirit is fully inhabiting your body, then you are inhabiting the whole universe.

Stay in tune with your body by being aware of how you dance with the universe. When walking, have awareness that you are walking. When sitting, have awareness that you are sitting. When breathing, have awareness that you are breathing. This is life-centered, present-moment awareness. Practice until you can stay anchored in this awareness and make it a permanent habit. Soon you will realize that in the dance of the universe, you are not walking; walking is happening. You are not sitting; sitting is happening. And you are not breathing; the one Being is breathing through you.

Pay Attention to the Rhythms and
Cycles of Your Body-Mind

Perhaps you can now understand, even scientifically, that your body is a whole universe within itself. Your body is the dance of the universe. So just saying, *My body is the dance of the universe,* is one of the most important things you can say to yourself.

If you understand the quantum mechanical nature of the body-mind, then you realize that the body is nothing other than vibrations in the unified field that result in the molecules that make up the body. The body is ultimately just vibration, and the vibration of the body has to match the vibrations that make up the universe. This matching, or falling into a rhythmic relationship with, is called *entrainment.*

Entrainment was first described by a physicist who did an interesting experiment with five clocks. Each clock had a pendulum about the same size, and he started the pendulums swinging at different times. After about four hours or so, the pendulums all started swinging synchronously to the same rhythm. You can do this experiment any number of times, and you'll find that even though you start the pendulums swinging at different times, after a while they all start swinging to the same rhythm.

Entrainment is a universal phenomenon, and it begins at the moment of conception. A baby's rhythms begin to entrain with cosmic rhythms through the physiology of the mother. Throughout the pregnancy, and even after the baby is born, the baby's heart rate will entrain with the mother's heart rate, and it keeps entraining as long as there is proximity to the mother. The heart rate may not be the same, but there is a rhythmic relationship between the two.

If you have a group of women living together, you find that after a while their menstrual cycles will entrain with one another. When you agree or disagree with somebody, you fall in or fall out of entrainment because your thoughts are stimulating the same quantum fields as their thoughts. When I agree with you, then my breathing spontaneously matches your breathing, and so on.

Your body is part of the body of the universe, and you can entrain your body's rhythms with the universal rhythms. How do you do this? You do it through your senses. What is sensory experience other than taking in information from the universe "outside" your body and matching it with the information "inside" your body, which is a universe within itself?

For example, if you introduce a sound that resonates in all the cells of your body, the vibration of the sound will facilitate entrainment. The sounds of the alphabet in all languages are tonal or vibrational sounds that can be used to immediately cause a vibration in all the cells of your body. In English, the sounds are A, E, I, O, U, and you can use any of these vowels to make a sound. Take a deep breath, and then as you exhale, make the sound of a vowel such as "Ahhhh," or "Ayyyy," or "Eeeee." As a result of this vibration, the cells begin to entrain with one another.

This is one way to restore biological rhythms, and to entrain your body's rhythms with universal rhythms. You can also do this with music you enjoy. Music influences your heart rate, brain waves, blood pressure, stomach contractions, and levels of hormones associated with stress. When you listen to music you enjoy, the body's pharmacy secretes endorphins, which are the body's natural opiates or morphine-like compounds. The body's pharmacy also generates healing neuropeptides when you listen to music you enjoy.

Your sense of sight also profoundly influences your body. Research has shown that information you take in through your eyes can influence heart rate, blood pressure, stress hormones, and so on. When you are looking at a natural scene such as a forest, or a sunset, or a rainbow, your brain waves show distinct patterns that are quite different from the patterns that appear when you are looking at an urban scene, an industrial plant, or a parking lot.

The sense of smell is another powerful way to evoke a pleasant sensation in the body. The smell of a rose or any fragrance that you enjoy can evoke a sense of harmony and joy. Certain aromas are known to stimulate the body-mind; others are known to calm and relax the body-mind. There are many books on the subject of aromatherapy, and you can experiment on your own with different aromas.

Any sensory input — whether you hear something, see something, smell something, taste something, or touch something — changes the body-mind's chemistry in less than a hundredth of a second. If we know that, then we can choose the appropriate input to influence the chemistry in a favorable direction.

Theoretically, if you were totally aligned with the cosmos, if you were in total harmony with its rhythms, and if you had zero stress, then there would be very little entropy in your body. Your body wouldn't age if you were totally synchronized with the cycles of the universe. If it did undergo entropy, it would be on the scale of the universe, which is cosmic cycles or eons of time. But your body-mind is not totally aligned with the rhythms of the universe, and why isn't it? Stress. You see, as soon as you have a thought, any thought, it interrupts the innate tendency of the biological rhythms to entrain with the universal rhythms.

But if you pay attention to the rhythms and cycles of your body-mind, and if you become a little familiar with cosmic rhythms, you'll see that you can synchronize your body's rhythms with the rhythms of the universe. You don't have to be an expert, just pay a little attention to this. Notice how you feel at different times of the day and at different times of the month depending on the lunar cycle. Look at the sky, and observe the cycles of the moon. If you look at a newspaper, check the high tide and low tide. Feel your body and see how it relates to each of the seasons. Understanding these rhythms can really help you, but the following information is all you need to remember.

Between six and ten in the morning and between six and ten in the evening is when your body is hypometabolic, or at its lowest phase of metabolism. Try to spend time in silence around six in the morning and six in the evening. Ideally speaking, it's best to meditate in the early part of this phase, and to exercise in the middle of this phase — especially if you're doing it to lose weight.

Between ten in the morning and two in the afternoon is when metabolic fire is at its highest. This is the time to have your biggest meal, because your body will metabolize the food much better. Between two and six in the afternoon is a good time to be active, to learn new mental skills, or to engage in physical activities. Between two and six in the morning is a good time to dream.

Around six in the evening, and preferably before sunset, is a good time to have dinner. It's best to make dinner a lighter meal, and to have at least a two- to three-hour interval between dinner and sleep. Then try to get to bed by ten or ten-thirty at night, and you'll have ideal sleep and great dreams.

These are very basic suggestions, but once you start to synchronize your rhythms with the cosmic rhythms, the body feels quite different. It feels vital; it doesn't get fatigued. You feel more energy subjectively. You begin to experience that state of consciousness where everything in your life is flowing with ease. And when everything is flowing with ease, you are living in the state of grace.

Vibrant health is not just the absence of disease; it's a joyfulness that should be inside you all the time. It's a state of positive well-being, which is not only physical but emotional, psychological, and ultimately even spiritual. Technology won't make you healthy. What *will* make you healthy is to be aligned with the forces of the universe, to feel that your body is part of the body of nature, to commune with nature, to commune with your soul, to take those moments of silence and solitude.

Your body is more than a life-support system; it is the expression of your soul on the journey of its evolution. The body is a sacred temple where you have stopped for a few moments on your cosmic journey. Keep this temple clean and pure. Listen to its cries for pleasure and even ecstasy. You are a privileged child of the universe, and this is your abode for now. The caravan of life will stop in other places, at other times. You are on a journey of healing and transformation, and the opportunity for your next quantum leap of creativity is right now.

∾

KEY POINTS

To experience and practice grace:

♦ Listen to your body's wisdom.

♦ Maintain inner-body awareness at all times.

♦ Pay attention to the rhythms and cycles of your body-mind.

· 12 ·

The Infinite

"The winds of grace are always blowing;
it is for us to raise our sails." — *Ramakrishna*

When my granddaughter was four years old, I took her for a walk on the beach. It was a beautiful night, and the stars and the moon were out. I turned to her and said, "Tara, I love you very much."

And as soon as I finished the sentence, she said, "How much?"

I said, "Well, I love you more than the stars and the moon."

And as soon as I finished the sentence, Tara said, "Why?"

I said, "Because you came from there."

And she said, "How?"

I thought to myself, *I don't know if I can explain this to her, but I'll try.* "You know, Tara, when you eat your fruits and vegetables, it's the light of the sun and the stars and the moon that made the food you eat. And when you eat the food, you're taking the light of the stars to make your body, because everything comes from the light. You are a being of light; your body is made out of light." Then I had another thought, and I said to her, "Even your eyes are made out of light. The stars made your eyes so they could see themselves."

Tara thought and she thought, and for the first time she was quiet. But as we were leaving the beach, she said, "Grandpa, look up. The stars want to see themselves."

And it's true. The infinite Being, the *one song*, which is the universe, moves and breathes and looks at itself through your body. The universe is looking at itself as the stars. The universe is looking at itself as the chair you sit upon. The universe is looking at itself as me, and it's looking at itself as you. We are the eyes and the ears of the universe. The universe looks, tastes, smells, feels, and hears itself in so many ways through each creature — through a honeybee, through a bird, through an antelope, through a butterfly.

If you could have just that little feeling of how the universe expresses itself through you, then you would be a better channel for that expression. There is nothing you cannot be or do or have, but you must get yourself, or what you think of as you, out of the way. It's just a shift in attitude, that's all.

Just allow the universe, the infinite, to express itself through you without interfering. Allow the infinite to see itself through you, to think itself through you, to experience itself through you. At the deepest level of your being, you are already powerful and free. When universal intelligence is flowing through you without interference, your life flows with effortless ease. This is the experience of grace.

Through your body-mind, you create and experience the world of objects and events in space-time. Through your intellect, you create and experience the world of ideas. Only through your soul can you create and experience the world of power, freedom, and grace. In the depths of your being is the light of pure Being, pure love, and pure joy. When you live from here, a new world opens. This world is unbounded, infinite, eternal, joyful. And this can be your world, if you want it. In this world, there's no limit to your power, freedom, and grace.

Understand the ideas in this book, follow the suggestions, and you will unlock the mysteries of your own existence. *Who are you? What do you want?* To know the answers to these questions is to know your true self. Once you know your true self, you will know true happiness, the intoxication of love, spirit flowing in its pure essence — unimpeded, unrestricted, full of mystery, magic, and adventure.

Happiness resides in the realm of spirit. To find happiness is to find your soul. To find your soul is to live from the source of lasting happiness. This is not happiness for this or that reason, which is just another form of misery. This happiness is true bliss, and it follows you wherever you go.

THE OLD AND NEW PARADIGMS

The following chart illustrates some of the old and new ways of perceiving ourselves and the world we live in. With the help of science, we are shifting into a new paradigm, not only of the human body-mind, but of our very interpretation of nature itself. This shift in our thinking sees the body-mind as an expression of a larger wholeness.

THE OLD PARADIGM	THE NEW PARADIGM
The superstition of materialism says that we are separate from our source and from one another.	The unified field of pure consciousness says that we are connected to our source and to one another.
The world is composed of visible, solid matter and invisible, nonmaterial energy.	The world is composed of one underlying, unmanifest field of intelligence that manifests as the infinite diversity of the universe.
Sensory experience — what we can see, hear, smell, taste, or touch — is the crucial test of reality.	The field of intelligence experienced subjectively is the mind; the same field experienced objectively is the world of material objects.

THE OLD PARADIGM	THE NEW PARADIGM
Solid objects, or visible clumps of matter, are separated from one another in space and time.	"Solid" objects are not solid at all, nor are they separate from one another in space and time. Objects are focal points, or concentrations of intelligence, within the field of intelligence.
Mind and matter are separate, independent entities.	Mind and matter are essentially the same. Both are the offspring of the field of pure consciousness, which conceives and constructs the whole world.
The body is a physical machine that has somehow learned how to think.	Infinite consciousness somehow creates the mind and then expresses itself as the body. The body-mind is the field of pure consciousness itself.
Human beings are self-contained entities with well-defined edges to the body.	Human beings are inseparably interconnected with the patterns of intelligence in the whole cosmos. At the most fundamental levels of nature, there are no well-defined edges between our personal body and the universe.

THE OLD PARADIGM	THE NEW PARADIGM
The human body is composed of matter frozen in space and time.	The human body-mind is a changing, pulsating pattern of intelligence that constantly re-creates itself.
Our needs are separate from the needs of other living beings.	Our needs are interdependent and inseparable from the needs of other living beings.
The external world is real because it is physical. Our internal world is unreal because it exists in the imagination.	The external world and the internal world are the projections of one Being, the source of all creation. Both are patterns of movement of energy within infinite consciousness.
The superstition of materialism says that we live in a local universe.	The unified field of pure consciousness says that we live in a nonlocal universe.
Location in space is an absolute phenomenon.	Everything in the cosmos is nonlocal, meaning we can't confine it to here, there, or anywhere.
Location in space exists independently of an observer.	Location in space is a matter of perception. Near or far, up or down, and east or west are only true from the vantage point of the observer.

THE OLD PARADIGM	THE NEW PARADIGM
The thinking mind is localized in the brain, and the body's intelligence is localized in the nervous system.	The thinking mind is part of a vast field of nonlocal intelligence that extends far beyond the reaches of the cosmos. The body's intelligence comes from the same nonlocal field.
The superstition of materialism says that we live in a time-bound universe.	The unified field of pure consciousness says that we live in a timeless universe.
Time is an absolute phenomenon.	Time is a relative phenomenon. Physicists no longer use the word *time;* they use the term *space-time continuum.*
Time is local, measurable, and limited.	Time is nonlocal, immeasurable, and eternal. The fact that we can localize time is just a notion, a perceptual artifact based on the quality of our attention.
Humans are entangled in a vast web of time that includes past, present, and future.	There is no past or future, then and now, before or after; there is only the eternal moment. Eternity extends backward and forward from every moment.

THE OLD PARADIGM	THE NEW PARADIGM
Time exists independently of an observer.	Time only exists in the mind of an observer. Time is a concept, an internal dialogue we use to explain our perception or experience of change.
Things happen one at a time. The world operates through linear cause-effect relationships.	Everything happens simultaneously, and everything is correlated and instantly synchronized with everything else.
How we interpret our experience of time has no effect on our physiology.	How we interpret our experience of time brings about physiological changes in our body. Entropy and aging are partly an expression of how we metabolize or interpret time.
The superstition of materialism says that we live in an objective universe.	The unified field of pure consciousness says that we live in a subjective universe.
The world "out there" is completely independent of an observer.	The world "out there" does not exist without an observer; it is a response of the observer. Through the act of observation, we construct the world we live in.

The Old Paradigm	The New Paradigm
Observation is an automatic phenomenon. Our senses are capable of interpreting an objective reality in an objective manner.	We live in a participatory universe. We learn to interpret the world through our senses, and this brings about our perceptual experiences.
Our inner world and our outer world are dependent upon our relationships, our environment, and the situations and circumstances around us.	Our inner world and our outer world interdependently co-arise depending on the level of vibration of our spirit.

Vedanta, one of the world's most ancient philosophies, is based on the Vedas and Upanishads, which are the earliest and most sacred scriptures of India. Regarded by many historians as the oldest surviving texts of humanity, these scriptures were said to be revealed by God rather than created by humans.

The word *veda* means knowledge, and the Vedas are considered to have existed since the beginning of creation. Centuries before they were written, the Vedas were passed on orally from teacher to student in the form of exact verses chanted in precise patterns of a three-note scale.

Vedanta tells us that our true nature is divine. The divine Self is the underlying reality and source of all that exists, and to realize this truth experientially is the goal of Vedanta. Revered for its enduring wisdom, Vedanta is a timeless philosophy that expresses the heart of all religions and spiritual doctrines.

∽

Deepak Chopra is a world-renowned leader in the fields of holistic health and human potential. He is a *New York Times* bestselling author of *The Seven Spiritual Laws of Success*, and numerous books and audio programs that cover every aspect of mind, body, and spirit. His books have been translated into more than fifty languages, and he travels widely throughout the world promoting peace, health, and well-being. Chopra is also the founder and executive director of The Chopra Center at La Costa Resort and Spa in Carlsbad, California.

For a complete list of books and audio programs by Deepak Chopra, or for information about ongoing seminars and other events, please visit:

www.deepakchopra.com

The Seven Spiritual Laws of Success by Deepak Chopra
Carry it with you in your purse or your pocket, and in less than one hour, learn the secrets to success in this *One Hour of Wisdom* edition of Chopra's classic bestseller.

Creating Affluence by Deepak Chopra
With clear and simple wisdom, Chopra explores the full meaning of wealth consciousness and offers A-to-Z steps that spontaneously generate wealth in all its forms.

Living Without Limits by Deepak Chopra and Wayne Dyer
Chopra and Dyer share their wisdom before a live audience as they question and challenge one another on the importance of quieting the inner dialogue, the power we have to heal ourselves of fatal diseases, and more. (Available in audio only.)

The Voice of Knowledge by don Miguel Ruiz
Ruiz reminds us of a profound and simple truth: The only way to end our emotional suffering and restore our joy in living is to stop believing in lies — mainly about ourselves.